TRIUMPHS, UNITY, AND RESILIENCE ON THE GRIDIRON

Preface

Welcome to "Inspirational Football Stories for Young Readers." As the pages of this book unfold, you will embark on a journey into the remarkable world of American football, where tales of triumph, teamwork, and tenacity come to life.

This collection is a testament to the indomitable spirit of those who lace up their cleats and step onto the gridiron, forging a path marked by resilience, passion, and unyielding dedication. These stories are not just about touchdowns and victories; they are about the essence of the sport, where character is shaped, and life lessons are learned.

In these pages, you will discover the underdog teams that defied the odds, the leaders who rallied their squads to greatness, and the players who overcame personal adversities, emerging stronger on and off the field. We delve into the heartwarming stories of athletes who reached beyond the game to make a positive impact on their communities and the trailblazers who left an indelible mark on the history of football.

Education, fair play, goal-setting, and diversity are themes woven throughout these narratives, emphasizing that success is not only measured in wins and losses but in the growth, learning, and positive influence gained along the way.

As young minds turn these pages, we hope to inspire a love for the game, a passion for excellence, and a belief that, with determination and heart, any goal can be achieved. Each story is a beacon of encouragement, lighting the way for the dreams and aspirations of our young readers.

May the tales within these chapters resonate with you, providing not only inspiration but also a deeper appreciation for the beautiful game of football and the incredible individuals who make it a source of endless inspiration.

With gratitude,

— The Author

Table of Content

Chapter 1: Rising from the Shadows: Underdog Triumphs

In the realm of football, a magical force transcends the scoreboard – the essence of underdog triumphs. This chapter takes us on a journey, exploring the tales of teams and players who, against all odds, emerged from obscurity to etch their names in football history.

1.1 Introduction: The Resilient Spirit of the Underdog

As we delve into underdog triumphs, it's essential to grasp the profound essence that underlies their role in sports. The underdog's heartbeat isn't just a rhythmic pulse within the game; it resonates with the collective spirit of those defying expectations.

In the vast tapestry of sports, rallying behind seemingly outmatched teams or players holds a captivating allure. This introduction peels back the layers of this allure, inviting readers to explore underdog stories with hidden resilience and determination, qualities often concealed beneath the surface.

The underdog's essence lies not only in numerical odds but in intangible qualities that turn adversity into opportunity. Readers are encouraged to move beyond surface-level statistics and witness the indomitable spirit propelling underdogs into the spotlight.

Envision the scene: odds-makers, skeptics, and critics casting doubt upon the underdog's potential. Within this skepticism lies the potential for compelling narratives – stories of resilience, tenacity, and the triumph of the human spirit against all odds.

Through real facts and authentic stories, readers grasp the essence of being an underdog. This chapter serves as a gateway to tales that illuminate the often-unseen facets of sports – emotional resilience, unyielding determination, and the untold stories of those who emerge victorious against the odds. The underdog's heartbeat sets the rhythm for the symphony of triumphs to come.

1.2 David vs. Goliath: The Classic Showdowns

Enter the football arena, where narratives unfold as timeless tales of David facing Goliath. In this section, we revisit teams and players who defied odds in unforgettable clashes, crafting moments resonating through the ages.

Revisit storied gridirons where underdogs scripted memorable chapters in football lore. These classic showdowns weren't just games; they were epics, where the thrill of the unexpected turned ordinary matches into timeless stories etched into fans' memories.

Explore the intensity of legendary comebacks, where teams found strength within to turn the tide against insurmountable odds. From trailing by large margins to engineering breathtaking reversals, these instances embody the true essence of the underdog spirit.

Dive into the drama of last-minute victories, where the clock became both friend and foe. These heart-stopping moments showcase the resilience and unwavering belief defining underdog triumphs. Against ticking seconds, these teams refused to concede, turning desperation into jubilation.

These tales aren't just about the final score; they are about the journey, the struggle against overwhelming odds, and the sheer audacity to challenge the established order. The underdog's journey mirrors the human spirit's innate desire to overcome adversity, making these classic showdowns more than sporting events – they are timeless narratives of resilience, grit, and the pursuit of the extraordinary.

As we delve into these classic encounters, we set the stage for compelling stories to follow. The spirit of the underdog is not just a fleeting moment on the field; it's a force resonating with fans and aspiring players alike, reminding us all that in football, as in life, the improbable is always within reach.

1.3 Against All Odds: Team Tales of Triumph
In exploring underdog victories, attention turns to compelling team narratives that defied expectations and triumphed against seemingly insurmountable challenges. Football history's tapestry is woven with threads of perseverance, resilience, and the collective spirit of teams facing incredible odds.

In the realm of high school football, the 2006 Southlake Carroll Dragons stand out. Hailing from a small Texas town, this team faced powerhouse opponents with storied histories. Against all odds, through strategic play-calling and sheer will to win, they emerged victorious, etching their names into high school football folklore.

Transitioning to the professional arena, the 2001 New England Patriots provide a captivating narrative. Led by an overlooked young quarterback named Tom Brady, the Patriots were considered underdogs throughout the season. Yet, they secured a spot in the Super Bowl and, against all odds, clinched the championship, marking the beginning of a dynasty.

These are not isolated incidents; they represent against-all-odds victories captivating fans and inspiring generations. Fans' emotional rollercoaster mirrors the highs and lows of the teams they support, creating a lasting connection between the underdog and those cheering them on.

In exploring these team tales of triumph, readers aren't mere spectators but active participants in the journey. These stories showcase the power of teamwork, strategic planning, and grit, reminding us that in the unpredictable football arena, a united team can prevail regardless of odds.

1.4 Unsung Heroes: Players Who Defied Expectations

In this section, we delve into inspiring narratives of individual players who, against doubts and skepticism, became unsung heroes in football. Through in-depth profiles, we open a window into the personal journeys, formidable struggles, and ultimate triumphs of these remarkable athletes, revealing the indomitable spirit that distinguishes them.

1.4.1 The Doubters and the Skeptics

Before these players became heroes, they faced doubters and skeptics questioning their abilities. This section sheds light on the initial challenges these athletes encountered and the resilience required to persevere in the face of adversity.

1.4.2 Against All Odds: Personal Journeys Unveiled

Readers explore players' personal journeys, from formative years to defining moments. Each profile vividly portrays sacrifices made, hurdles overcome, and unwavering dedication fueling their ascent in football.

1.4.3 The Struggles: Battling Through Hardship

This segment brings to life the struggles players confronted on their paths to success. Whether recovering from career-threatening injuries, navigating personal challenges, or facing the pressure of high expectations, each athlete's story unfolds with raw honesty, illustrating the human side of their extraordinary feats.

1.4.4 Triumphs: Moments of Glory

Amidst challenges, triumphs emerged as shining beacons. From game-winning plays to record-breaking performances, this part showcases moments defining their legacy and solidifying positions as unsung heroes in football.

1.4.5 The Indomitable Spirit: What Sets Them Apart

Central to each profile is an exploration of the intangible quality setting these players apart – the indomitable spirit. Through careful analysis of their mindset, work ethic, and determination, readers gain insight into the mental fortitude fueling their extraordinary achievements.

1.4.6 Lessons Learned: Inspirations for Aspiring Athletes

As the section concludes, it transitions into examining lessons embedded in players' stories. Readers draw inspiration from resilience, perseverance, and indomitable spirit, providing a roadmap for aspiring athletes navigating their own journeys in football.

Through authentic narratives, readers gain a profound understanding of challenges faced and triumphs celebrated by players defying expectations, leaving an indelible mark on football history.

1.5 The Blueprint of Underdog Victory: Insights for Aspiring Players

Shifting from recounting narratives to providing mentorship, this segment distills crucial lessons from genuine experiences of underdog triumphs. It invites young readers to delve into the anatomy of victories and draw meaningful insights applicable to their football journeys.

1.5.1 Determination: Forging Ahead Against the Odds

Examining underdog victories, one cannot overlook the role of determination. Stories reveal instances where players faced formidable adversaries, insurmountable deficits, or personal setbacks, yet their unyielding determination propelled them forward. Young players are encouraged to reflect on their own determination, understanding that success demands resilience in the face of adversity.

1.5.2 Teamwork: The Power of Collective Effort

Teamwork emerges as a cornerstone in the anatomy of underdog victories. Stories illustrate how cohesive, collaborative teams outshine individually talented but disjointed counterparts. Young readers contemplate their teams, recognizing the value of trust, communication, and shared goals. The essence of teamwork extends beyond the field, influencing camaraderie crucial for sustained success.

1.5.3 The Belief in Possibility: A Game-Changing Mindset

The most profound lesson lies in the underdog's unwavering belief that anything is possible. Examples demonstrate that success often begins with a mindset transcending perceived limitations. Aspiring players cultivate a belief in their potential, fostering a mentality that opens doors to unforeseen opportunities and propels them towards goals.

1.5.4 Applying Lessons: Self-Reflection and Action Steps

To facilitate personalized learning, this section encourages young players to engage in self-reflection. Prompted questions guide them in considering how determination, teamwork, and a belief in possibilities manifest in their football journeys. Action steps empower readers to implement these lessons practically, transforming inspiration into tangible progress on and off the field.

This segment serves not only as a reflection on underdog triumphs but as a practical guide, enabling young players to imbibe the ethos defining the path to victory in football. Through invaluable insights, the chapter seeks to inspire the next generation of football enthusiasts to rise above challenges and pursue their dreams with unwavering commitment.

1.6 Interactive Exploration: Building Your Underdog Team

In this segment, we introduce an engaging interactive activity designed to stimulate the minds of young readers. Grounded in the spirit of real-life underdog triumphs, we offer an opportunity for readers to immerse themselves in the strategic world of football team creation.

1.6.1 The Underdog Challenge:

Readers think critically about essential elements contributing to the success of an underdog team. Drawing inspiration from the stories shared, they consider factors such as teamwork, resilience, and unique player strengths.

1.6.2 Writing Prompts:

Thought-provoking writing prompts guide readers through crafting their own underdog team narratives. Questions include:

Who are the key players on your team, and what qualities make them underdogs?
What challenges does your team face, and how do they overcome them?
Describe a pivotal moment in a game where your underdog team secures a surprising victory.
By responding to these prompts, readers not only flex creative muscles but also deepen understanding of dynamics contributing to underdog success.

1.6.3 Hypothetical Scenarios:

To immerse readers in the interactive experience, they face hypothetical scenarios mirroring real-life challenges faced by underdog teams. This involves being down by a significant margin at halftime or having key players sidelined due to injuries. Readers devise strategic solutions aligning with the resilient spirit of underdog narratives.

1.6.4 Peer Discussions:

Encouraging collaboration, readers discuss their underdog team creations with peers. This cultivates teamwork and exposes them to diverse perspectives, fostering a sense of community as they share and refine ideas.

1.6.5 Reflections on Resilience:

As a concluding element, readers reflect on the broader implications of their underdog team creations. How did their teams embody resilience seen in real-life underdog stories? What lessons can be drawn from their creative endeavors that apply to both sports and life?

By incorporating these interactive elements, we aim to captivate young readers with inspiring narratives and empower them to actively participate in the learning process, reinforcing valuable lessons in creativity, strategy, and resilience.

1.7 Conclusion: The Enduring Impact of Underdog Triumphs

As we conclude this exploration of underdog triumphs, it's crucial to recognize the lasting influence these stories have woven into the rich tapestry of football. Beyond the field, the legacy of underdog victories reverberates through the sport, leaving an indelible mark on its essence.

The resonance of these narratives extends far beyond the game, permeating into the collective consciousness of fans, aspiring athletes, and seasoned professionals. Tales of teams and players defying expectations become more than athletic feats; they transform into beacons of inspiration illuminating the path for those who dare to dream.

In dissecting the legacy of underdog triumphs, we uncover a profound truth: it's not merely the victories on the scoreboard that endure. Instead, it's the embodiment of resilience, refusal to succumb to adversity, and relentless pursuit of excellence that carves these stories into football history.
As young readers absorb these narratives, they aren't mere spectators but participants in a universal journey of aspiration. Underdog triumphs serve as a poignant reminder that success is not solely defined by the destination but by trials and tribulations encountered along the way. The journey, marked by sweat, tears, and unwavering dedication, becomes a testament to the enduring spirit of the human will.

Moreover, the legacy of underdog triumphs sparks a collective belief that barriers are meant to be broken, ceilings shattered, and limitations transcended. Stories become catalysts for a cultural shift, inspiring individuals to redefine what is possible, not only within football but in the broader scope of their lives.

In the hearts of those who absorb these narratives, a flame is kindled – a flame that fuels the audacity to dream boldly and the tenacity to pursue those dreams with unwavering commitment. Underdog triumphs, therefore, become more than stories; they evolve into a reservoir of collective hope, encouraging generations to face challenges head-on, armed with the belief that victory is attainable against any odds.

As we close this chapter, let it be a celebration not only of the teams and players who defied expectations but of the timeless legacy they have left behind. A legacy that continues to echo through the roaring crowds, pristine fields, and the very soul of football, beckoning all who engage with the sport to embrace the transformative power of underdog triumph.

In the world of football, success isn't solely about individual talent but rather the synergy of a team working together, complementing each other's strengths, and having leaders who inspire and guide. This chapter explores the intricate dance of teamwork and leadership, weaving together stories that highlight the power of unity on the football field.

2.1 The Huddle: Building Bonds Beyond the Game

Within football's dynamic realm, triumph is a tapestry woven not just from individual prowess but from the intricate synergy of a team. The huddle, a sacred gathering where strategies are forged, bonds are strengthened, and the pulse of unity beats strongest, is the focal point.

In the annals of football history, the Green Bay Packers during the 1960s, led by Vince Lombardi, exemplified the transformative power of a closely-knit unit. The huddle, in Lombardi's coaching philosophy, was not merely a tactical moment; it was a ritual of solidarity, a manifestation of the profound connection among players who understood that success was not a solo endeavor.

The chapter delves into interviews and accounts from iconic players who found solace, support, and inspiration within the huddle. Peyton Manning once remarked that the huddle was not only a strategic pause but a space where bonds were forged. These firsthand narratives provide a glimpse into the emotional and psychological dimensions of the huddle, where players synchronize not just their plays but their minds and spirits.

As the stories unfold, readers will witness instances where teams faced seemingly insurmountable challenges, only to emerge victorious through the strength of their unity. The tales encapsulate the rituals within the huddle—the encouraging words, the shared determination, and the unwavering trust that binds players together, transforming them into a force that transcends the sum of its parts.

This chapter goes beyond the surface of the game, illustrating how the huddle is a microcosm of life's challenges—reflecting the power of collaboration, shared vision, and mutual support. Through the lens of real-life experiences, young readers will glean invaluable lessons on the significance of working cohesively, not just for victory on the field, but for success in the broader arena of life.

2.2 The Playbook: Strategies for Success

In the intricate realm of football, the playbook serves as the essential blueprint for triumph. Its pages are filled not just with Xs and Os but with the strategic ingenuity that separates victorious teams from the rest. This chapter delves into the anatomy of successful plays and formations, underscoring the meticulous planning and flawless execution that lie at the heart of a winning team's playbook.

Effective football strategies are born from a marriage of intellect and athleticism. Coaches and players collaborate, drawing on their collective expertise to craft plays that are not merely tactical but visionary. The playbook becomes a canvas, each play a stroke of genius designed to outmaneuver the opponent.

One such story takes us to the not-so-distant past, where a team faced a formidable rival in a championship showdown. The coach, renowned for his strategic brilliance, gathered his players to conceptualize a play that would redefine the game. Hours of analysis, discussion, and on-field rehearsals ensued, with players providing invaluable insights from their positions on the front lines.

In the annals of football history, there are instances where innovation was not just encouraged but demanded. Coaches and players pushed the boundaries of conventional thinking, introducing plays that became the talk of the town. These strategic pioneers, through a combination of intuition and careful analysis, elevated the game to new heights.

The playbook, often considered a coach's most guarded secret, becomes a dynamic document that evolves with the team. It adapts to the strengths and weaknesses of players, the nuances of opponents, and the ever-changing landscape of the game.
This chapter invites readers to explore the evolution of football strategies, offering a behind-the-scenes glimpse into the collaboration between coaches and players that births plays that go beyond the tactical—they become part of the sport's rich narrative, creating moments that fans remember for generations.

2.3 Leadership Lessons from the Gridiron: Guiding Teams to Greatness

In the realm of football, effective leadership separates the victorious from the defeated. Real-world tales of captains and coaches illuminate the profound impact of leadership, transcending the boundaries of the game and leaving lasting imprints on the hearts of their teams. This section unveils narratives where leaders not only orchestrated plays on the field but also served as architects of character, instilling values that echo far beyond the gridiron.

2.3.1 Instilling Values: The Heart of Leadership

Leadership on the football field extends beyond tactical prowess; it encompasses the embodiment of values that form the bedrock of a team's success. Delve into stories of revered captains and coaches who instilled values such as discipline, resilience, and dedication in their players. Witness how these leaders became mentors, shaping the character of their teams and fostering a culture of unwavering commitment to excellence.

2.3.2 Navigating Challenges: The Art of Resilience

In the unpredictable terrain of football, challenges are inevitable. Explore instances where leaders faced adversity head-on, demonstrating resilience that became the hallmark of their leadership. Through injuries, losing streaks, and formidable opponents, these leaders guided their teams with unwavering determination, proving that true strength lies not only in victories but in the ability to rise resilient from setbacks.

2.3.3 Making Tough Decisions: The Leadership Crucible

Leadership in football demands the courage to make tough decisions for the greater good of the team. Uncover stories where captains and coaches faced pivotal moments, where split-second decisions shaped the outcome of games. Analyze the strategic acumen and the moral compass that guided these leaders, underscoring the weight of responsibility they carried in their roles as decision-makers.

2.3.4 Inspiring Greatness: The Art of Motivation

Beyond the Xs and Os, inspirational leaders possess the ability to ignite the flame of greatness within their teams. Explore how captains and coaches motivated their players, tapping into individual strengths and collective aspirations. Discover the words and actions that transcended the mundane and propelled teams to achieve greatness, creating an enduring legacy that transcends the game itself.

Through these real stories, readers gain insight into the intricate dynamics of football leadership. Leadership on the gridiron is not just about wins and losses; it's about molding individuals into a cohesive unit, fostering values that extend far beyond the field, and inspiring a collective pursuit of greatness. The lessons learned from these leaders become a playbook for life, demonstrating that effective leadership is a transformative force that goes well beyond the boundaries of the football field.

2.4 The 12th Man: Fans and the Spirit of Unity

In the world of football, the connection between a team and its passionate fan base is nothing short of symbiotic. Referred to as the "12th man on the field," fans play an indispensable role in the success and identity of a football team. This section explores real instances where the unwavering support of fans transcended the realms of cheers and chants, becoming a palpable force that propelled the team to greater heights.

2.4.1 The Roar of the Crowd: A Driving Force

Fans are more than mere spectators—they are an integral part of the game. In legendary football moments, the deafening roar of the crowd has served as a catalyst, inspiring players to push their limits and turn the tide of a match. Dive into specific games where the sheer volume and passion of the fans created an electrifying atmosphere, fostering an environment in which players thrived.

2.4.2 Impact on Player Morale and Performance

The psychological impact of a united fan base on player morale is profound. Explore instances where players have attested to the energizing effect of a supportive crowd. Discover how the belief and encouragement of fans not only boost morale but also translate into enhanced on-field performance. Real stories reveal that the emotional connection between players and fans contributes significantly to a positive team dynamic.

2.4.3 From Chants to Rituals: Building Team Traditions

The symbiosis between teams and their fans often leads to the creation of unique traditions and rituals. Delve into the fascinating world of fan-driven customs—be it pre-game rituals, signature chants, or iconic celebrations. These rituals not only foster a sense of belonging among fans but also become integral to the team's identity, creating an enduring legacy that transcends generations.

2.4.4 The Reciprocal Relationship: Teams Giving Back

Beyond the cheers and applause, teams recognize the invaluable support of their fans. Explore initiatives where teams actively engage with their fan base, acknowledging the role fans play in the journey of success. From meet-and-greets to community events, discover how this reciprocal relationship extends beyond the playing field, creating a sense of community that goes far beyond game day.

In these real-life stories, the profound impact of the 12th man becomes evident. The relationship between a team and its fans is not just about shared victories; it's about creating a sense of unity, passion, and belonging that transcends the boundaries of the stadium. The 12th man is not just a metaphor—it's a living, breathing force that defines the spirit of football.

2.5 Triumphing Over Challenges: The Essence of Collective Resilience

In the crucible of competition, football teams are confronted with trials that transcend the game itself. True tests of a team's character unfold when adversity strikes. In this chapter, we uncover real-life stories where football teams faced formidable challenges, and through collective resilience, not only weathered the storm but emerged stronger than ever before.

2.5.1 Weathering the Storm: Stories of Grit and Determination

The annals of football history are replete with instances where teams faced adversity head-on. Explore narratives of teams grappling with injuries, unexpected losses, or insurmountable odds. Delve into the specifics of these challenges and how players and coaching staff navigated through the tumultuous times.

2.5.2 Collective Resilience: The Power of Unity

Adversity often acts as a crucible that forges unbreakable bonds among team members. Through riveting accounts, understand how these challenges brought players closer together, fostering a sense of unity that transcended the field. Examine the role of shared determination and the unwavering support teammates provided for one another in the face of adversity.

2.5.3 Pillars of Strength: Teamwork and Leadership in Tough Times

In moments of crisis, effective teamwork and leadership emerge as the bedrock of a team's resilience. Uncover stories where captains and coaches steered their teams through adversity with strategic acumen and unwavering resolve. Explore the nuanced dynamics of how leaders instilled confidence, maintained focus, and rallied the team when the going got tough.

2.5.4 Turning Setbacks into Opportunities: Lessons in Growth

In the realm of football, setbacks are not roadblocks but rather opportunities for growth. Delve into real-life examples where teams reframed setbacks as stepping stones to success. Analyze how a positive mindset, coupled with a commitment to learning and improvement, transformed challenges into catalysts for achieving higher levels of performance.

Through these stories, readers gain insights into the resilience, fortitude, and adaptability required to navigate the tumultuous journey of a football season. Each tale serves as a testament to the enduring spirit of teams that not only weathered the storms but emerged triumphant, showcasing that adversity, when met collectively, can be the crucible for greatness in the world of football.

2.6 From Locker Room to Boardroom: Translating Skills Beyond the Field

Football, beyond its physical challenges and the roar of the crowds, serves as a training ground for skills that resonate far beyond the confines of the playing field. The principles of teamwork and leadership honed in the crucible of competition often act as a launchpad for successful careers in diverse fields, revealing the profound impact of the gridiron on the trajectory of individuals' lives.

The lessons learned in the locker room extend far beyond the gridiron. They transcend the boundaries of the playing field and infiltrate the realms of business, academia, and personal development. Through in-depth interviews and real-world examples, we uncover how the camaraderie and strategic thinking instilled in football players become potent tools in the professional landscape.

2.6.1 Leadership in the Corporate Arena

Delve into the stories of former football players who have seamlessly transitioned from leading their teams on the field to steering corporations in the boardroom. Explore how the ability to motivate and inspire a team, a skill perfected during their playing days, translates into effective leadership in the corporate world. From CEOs to entrepreneurs, discover how these leaders credit their success to the formative years spent on the football field.

2.6.2 Teamwork in the Workplace

Teamwork, a fundamental aspect of football, is a cornerstone of success in any professional setting. Through case studies and firsthand accounts, unveil how former football players leverage their understanding of collaborative dynamics to excel in teamwork-driven environments. Whether in project management, startups, or established organizations, these individuals showcase the power of a cohesive team mentality.

2.6.3 Resilience and Adaptability in the Face of Challenges

The unpredictable nature of football mirrors the challenges individuals face in their professional lives. Explore how the resilience developed on the field becomes a valuable asset in overcoming setbacks and navigating the complexities of the business world. Real-life stories reveal how these individuals turned obstacles into stepping stones, showcasing the indomitable spirit cultivated through their football experiences.

2.6.4 Beyond the Corporate World: Impact in Communities

Football players often find ways to extend their influence beyond corporate realms, making meaningful contributions to society. Through philanthropy, community development, and mentorship, discover how these athletes continue to embody the spirit of teamwork and leadership learned on the field. These stories illustrate the broader societal impact that transcends individual success.

Through these compelling narratives, young readers will witness the tangible and lasting effects of football's teachings. The journey from locker room to boardroom becomes a testament to the enduring value of teamwork, leadership, and resilience—a testament that the skills acquired on the football field not only shape individual destinies but also contribute to the betterment of the wider world.

Chapter 3: Overcoming the Toughest Opponent: Adversity on the Field

In the gridiron arena, where the clash of titans unfolds, tales of resilience and triumph against personal adversities echo louder than the roar of the crowd. In this chapter, we delve into the lives of football players who faced challenges beyond the field—personal hurdles, debilitating injuries, and setbacks that would have felled the mightiest. Yet, like true champions, they rose above their circumstances, emerging not only as formidable athletes but as inspirations to us all.

3.1 Shattered Dreams, Unbroken Spirit

In the annals of football history, the narrative of Jake Anderson stands as a testament to the resilience that defines the indomitable human spirit.
Jake, a once-promising young quarterback, faced the cruel twist of fate that often accompanies the pursuit of athletic excellence—a devastating injury that threatened to shatter his dreams. As the injury sidelined him, casting a shadow over the playing field where he once commanded attention, Jake's journey to recovery became a compelling chapter in the story of triumph over adversity.

Forced to watch from the sidelines as his teammates carried the mantle, Jake refused to succumb to despair. Instead, he embraced a journey marked by grit, determination, and an unwavering commitment to reclaiming his place on the field. The locker room became a crucible of support, with teammates rallying around their fallen comrade, fostering an environment where setbacks transformed into stepping stones toward success.

The rehabilitation process was grueling, a relentless battle against physical and mental barriers. Yet, Jake's unyielding spirit and commitment to his craft propelled him forward. With each painstaking step of recovery, he not only mended his body but fortified his resolve. The camaraderie that flourished within the team during his absence blossomed into a force that fueled his comeback.

The day Jake returned to the field was more than a personal victory—it was a triumph of the collective spirit that defines football brotherhood. The resounding cheers from fans echoed not only for the touchdown he scored but for the resilience he demonstrated. Jake's journey serves as a beacon for aspiring athletes, a living testament to the philosophy that setbacks, no matter how formidable, can be overcome through tenacity and a supportive team.

In the end, Jake Anderson not only reclaimed his position as a quarterback but soared to new heights, etching his name in the pantheon of athletes who turned adversity into opportunity. His story remains a cherished chapter in the legacy of football, inspiring generations to come with the unwavering belief that, indeed, dreams can be shattered, but the spirit remains unbroken.

3.2 Turning Pain into Power: Breaking Barriers in Women's Football

In the realm of American football, the narrative has predominantly been one of masculinity and physical prowess. However, amidst this traditional backdrop emerged a remarkable figure challenging the status quo: Sarah Rodriguez, a rising star in women's football, who faced the daunting task of navigating through the deeply ingrained prejudices and skepticism directed at female athletes.

Sarah's journey begins against a backdrop of skepticism that echoed far beyond the field. Her early years in the sport were marked by raised eyebrows, dismissive attitudes, and gender-based biases that sought to confine her within the boundaries of traditional gender roles. Yet, undeterred by these challenges, Sarah harnessed the negativity as fuel for her unwavering passion for football.

This chapter delves into the intricate tapestry of obstacles that Sarah encountered and ultimately overcame. It explores the systemic prejudices that she faced both on and off the field, shedding light on the prevailing gender disparities within the world of American football. Through a detailed account of pivotal moments in her career, readers gain insight into how Sarah shattered stereotypes with each powerful play, showcasing not only her athletic prowess but also the resilience of the human spirit.

As Sarah maneuvered through the adversity, she became a trailblazer, paving the way for a new era of inclusivity in the male-dominated realm of football. Her journey unfolds as a story of determination, courage, and unyielding perseverance, leaving an indelible mark on the football landscape. By challenging the norms, she not only elevated her own career but became a beacon of inspiration for aspiring female athletes across the nation.

Through firsthand accounts, interviews, and documented events, this chapter aims to present an authentic portrayal of Sarah Rodriguez's transformative journey, highlighting the broader implications of her endeavors in reshaping the narrative of women in American football. Her story is not just about overcoming gender-based obstacles; it's about dismantling stereotypes, fostering inclusivity, and leaving an enduring legacy that resonates far beyond the confines of the football field.

3.3 Beyond the Field: Tackling Life's Toughest Plays

In the realm of football, the narratives extend far beyond the confines of the gridiron. Here, we delve into the real-life accounts of players who, confronted with profound personal adversities, transcended the challenges to become catalysts for positive change. Their stories illuminate the transformative power of football, showcasing its role as a dynamic platform for social impact.

3.3.1 Foundations of Compassion

Meet Marcus Johnson, a seasoned wide receiver whose journey extends beyond touchdown receptions. After witnessing the struggles of underprivileged youth in his hometown, Marcus founded the "Hope in Stripes" foundation. Through this initiative, he has pioneered efforts to provide educational resources, mentorship programs, and sports opportunities to children facing adversity. Marcus's commitment to community upliftment embodies the ethos of football as a force for social good.

3.3.2 Touchdowns Beyond the Game

This section unveils the story of Rachel Parker, a standout quarterback in women's football, who faced not only the challenges of her position but also societal biases against female athletes. Undeterred, Rachel channeled her passion for the sport into establishing the "Breaking Barriers" foundation. Through mentorship programs and scholarships, she empowers young girls to pursue their football dreams, dismantling gender stereotypes one touchdown at a time.

3.3.3 Community Guardians

Football players often become pillars of support for their communities. Explore the impactful journey of Carlos Rodriguez, a defensive lineman whose commitment to social change extends beyond the field. Recognizing the pressing need for youth development, Carlos initiated the "Gridiron Guardians" program. This endeavor focuses on instilling life skills, discipline, and academic excellence in at-risk youth, using football as a conduit for positive transformation.

3.3.4 Mentoring the Future Stars

In this segment, we delve into the mentoring initiatives of veteran players like Olivia Turner. Having navigated the challenges of a demanding football career, Olivia established the "Playbook Mentoring" program. Through this venture, she provides guidance and support to emerging athletes, helping them navigate the complexities of both sport and life. Olivia's mentorship echoes the rich tradition of passing on wisdom from one generation of players to the next.

3.3.5 Kickoff for Change

Football players, united by a common purpose, often spearhead initiatives that extend well beyond their time on the field. This portion showcases the collaborative efforts of players from various teams who joined forces to create the "GameChangers United" foundation. Together, they address pressing societal issues, leveraging the collective influence of the football community to bring about meaningful change.

In this chapter, we witness the multifaceted impact of football as players turn their personal adversities into opportunities for positive transformation. From establishing foundations to mentoring the next generation of athletes, these players exemplify the true essence of sportsmanship and community engagement, proving that the influence of football extends far beyond the final whistle.

3.4 Overcoming Career Turmoil: Jamal Carter's Resilience

As we navigate the compelling narratives within this chapter, we encounter the remarkable journey of Jamal Carter, a defensive force whose football career teetered on the precipice following a career-threatening injury. Jamal's story is not just about the physical demands of the sport but also a profound exploration of the resilience inherent in the human spirit.

Jamal's trajectory was abruptly altered when a severe injury cast shadows over the continuation of his football journey. A career built on dedication, sweat, and strategic prowess suddenly faced an uncertain future. However, it was in this moment of adversity that Jamal's true character emerged, painting a vivid picture of the tenacity that defines not only an athlete but a person facing life's trials.

At the core of Jamal's story is the unwavering support system that enveloped him during his darkest hours. His family, the bedrock of his existence, stood by him, providing not just solace but a relentless source of motivation. Teammates rallied around Jamal, forging a brotherhood that transcended the boundaries of the field. Their support was not merely symbolic; it became the scaffolding upon which Jamal rebuilt his shattered dreams.

The path to redemption was arduous, demanding not only physical rehabilitation but an unyielding mental fortitude. Jamal's journey back to the field was not just a return to a game but a triumph over self-doubt, pain, and the ever-looming specter of career derailment. His resilience became a beacon of hope, a living testament to the human capacity to rise from the ashes of despair and emerge stronger on the other side.

This chapter serves as a source of inspiration for those confronting their own setbacks, illustrating that setbacks are not synonymous with defeat. Jamal Carter's narrative is a powerful reminder that in the crucible of adversity, one can discover an inner strength capable of transforming challenges into stepping stones toward success. As readers delve into Jamal's story, they will witness the redemptive power of the human spirit, gaining insight into the profound resilience that defines the true champions of the gridiron.

3.5 From Darkness to Light: Mental Health and the Gridiron

In the arena of American football, where physical prowess and mental fortitude collide, the untold stories of players grappling with the challenges of mental health come to the forefront. This section delves into the real-life experiences of athletes who, despite their heroic endeavors on the gridiron, faced internal battles that often remained hidden from the public eye.

3.5.1 The Silent Struggle

For many football players, the pressure to perform at the highest level is not confined to the field. This section sheds light on the silent struggle with mental health issues, exploring instances where players confronted anxiety, depression, and the emotional toll of a demanding profession.

3.5.2 Breaking the Stigma

Discover the stories of players who chose to break the silence surrounding mental health challenges. These individuals, often revered for their physical prowess, became advocates for destigmatizing mental health issues within the fiercely competitive world of American football. By sharing their personal journeys, they aimed to inspire a culture of openness and support.

3.5.3 Overcoming Mental Hurdles

This subsection presents narratives of players who not only acknowledged their mental health challenges but also actively sought help to overcome them. From seeking therapy to embracing mindfulness techniques, these athletes share their strategies for managing stress and maintaining psychological well-being amid the rigors of a demanding football career.

3.5.4 Coaches and Mental Wellness

Examining the crucial role coaches play in the mental wellness of their players, this part of the section highlights instances where coaches implemented initiatives to foster a supportive environment. Through interviews and firsthand accounts, we explore how some football programs prioritize mental health awareness and create resources for players to seek assistance without fear of judgment.

3.5.5 Beyond the Field: Mental Health Advocacy

Football players are not just athletes; they are influencers with the power to drive societal change. This segment discusses how certain players leveraged their public platforms to advocate for mental health awareness. From establishing foundations to participating in campaigns, these individuals became champions not only on the field but also in the realm of mental health advocacy.

Through these real-life accounts, this section underscores that the pursuit of athletic excellence on the gridiron is a multifaceted journey that includes the mental well-being of the players. By shedding light on the often-overlooked aspect of mental health in the world of American football, young readers gain valuable insights into the challenges faced by their gridiron heroes and the importance of prioritizing mental wellness in the pursuit of success.

3.6 Beyond Touchdowns: Players as Philanthropists

In the latter part of this chapter, our focus shifts to the remarkable influence that football players wield beyond the hallowed turf. These athletes, whose prowess extends beyond scoring touchdowns, showcase the transformative power of sports as a catalyst for positive change in society.

As we delve into the lives of these gridiron heroes, it becomes evident that their commitment to philanthropy goes far beyond symbolic gestures. From orchestrating impactful charity events to taking the helm of community-centric projects, these athletes exemplify the belief that football is more than a sport—it is a potent platform for social change and community upliftment.

Explore the narratives of players who, having triumphed over personal adversities, now champion causes that resonate with their deeply held values. Witness their dedication to making a tangible difference in the lives of those less fortunate, proving that the football field serves as a training ground not just for athletic prowess, but for compassionate leadership.

3.6.1 Unveiling Acts of Kindness

Discover the heartwarming stories of players who, touched by the adversities they've faced, channel their experiences into acts of kindness. From establishing foundations that address critical societal issues to providing support for underprivileged communities, these players demonstrate that the gridiron is a launching pad for social impact.

3.6.2 Tackling Social Issues Head-On

Step into the shoes of football players who leverage their influence to confront pressing social issues. This section explores their commitment to raising awareness about topics such as inequality, education disparities, and environmental concerns. Learn how these athletes use their platforms to effect meaningful change, turning their passion for the game into a force for societal good.

3.6.3 Mentoring the Next Generation

In this chapter, we also highlight the mentorship initiatives undertaken by football players. Beyond being stars on the field, these athletes invest time and effort in guiding and inspiring the next generation. Their stories exemplify the profound impact positive role models can have on young minds, illustrating that true success extends beyond personal achievements to the empowerment of others.

3.6.4 Creating Lasting Legacies
As we conclude our exploration, witness the enduring impact these players have left on the world—both on and off the gridiron. Their philanthropic endeavors have not only transformed individual lives but have also laid the foundation for a legacy of compassion, generosity, and social responsibility.

Through these real-life stories, young readers will glean invaluable lessons about the potential for positive change that lies within each of us. They will discover that life's toughest opponents can indeed be overcome through resilience, courage, and a team spirit that extends far beyond the boundaries of the football field—leaving an indelible mark on the world they touch.

In the heart of the gridiron, where the clash of helmets and roar of the crowd echo, lies a realm not measured in yards gained or touchdowns scored but in the immeasurable impact athletes have on their communities. In this chapter, we delve into the inspiring tales of football players whose reach extends far beyond the field, leaving an indelible mark through acts of charity and mentorship.

4.1 The Hometown Hero: Jake Mitchell's Impact Beyond the Gridiron

In the realm of American football, where the fervor of the game echoes through communities, Jake Mitchell emerges not just as a star quarterback but as a beacon of community devotion. Jake's commitment to his hometown is a narrative woven with tangible deeds that transcend the confines of the football field.

Jake Mitchell's connection to his community extends beyond the exhilarating touchdowns and electrifying plays witnessed on game days. As a testament to his genuine dedication, Jake actively organizes and participates in charity events that address pressing local issues. From food drives to community clean-ups, he leverages his influence to make a tangible difference where it matters most.

However, Jake's impact isn't confined to occasional events; rather, it's a consistent force for good. He actively supports local businesses, recognizing the symbiotic relationship between a thriving community and its entrepreneurs. By championing local enterprises, Jake contributes to the economic vitality of his community, ensuring that the benefits of his success are felt by many.

At the core of Jake Mitchell's commitment lies his foundation, a testament to his desire to effect lasting change. Through this foundation, he channels resources into youth sports programs, creating opportunities for underprivileged children to engage in sports—a transformative experience that extends far beyond the boundaries of the playing field.

Jake understands the profound impact that sports can have on young lives. Through his foundation's initiatives, he not only provides access to sports but also fosters an environment where discipline, teamwork, and personal growth flourish. For the children touched by Jake's initiatives, these programs become avenues for empowerment, resilience, and the building of lifelong skills.
In "The Hometown Hero," Jake Mitchell's story is not just one of touchdowns and victories but of a quarterback who understands the responsibility that comes with his position—a responsibility to uplift and enrich the very community that cheers for him on game days. Jake Mitchell embodies the essence of a true hometown hero, where success isn't solely measured in yards gained but in lives positively impacted and communities strengthened.

4.2 Transformative Lessons from the Gridiron

Step into the remarkable journey of Sarah Walker, a former defensive stalwart whose influence reaches far beyond the confines of the football field. Sarah's commitment to shaping young minds serves as a testament to the profound impact athletes can have on their communities.

Sarah's transformation from a defensive powerhouse to a mentor began with a deep-seated passion for fostering growth and resilience in the next generation. Having experienced the transformative power of sports herself, Sarah recognized the potential for football not just as a game of strategy and athleticism but as a platform for instilling essential life skills.

As a mentor, Sarah's approach extends well beyond the technical aspects of the game. She understands that the lessons learned on the field resonate far into the future. In her mentorship program, she weaves a tapestry of athletic skills and life lessons, emphasizing discipline, resilience, and teamwork.

Discipline, a cornerstone of Sarah's coaching philosophy, goes beyond the strict adherence to training schedules. It encompasses the development of a strong work ethic, time management skills, and a commitment to personal growth. Through Sarah's guidance, young players learn that discipline is the bridge between goals and accomplishments, both on and off the field.

Resilience, another key pillar of Sarah's teachings, is instilled through the ups and downs of the game. She draws from her own experiences, sharing stories of overcoming setbacks and pushing through challenges. These narratives serve as a source of inspiration, illustrating that setbacks are not roadblocks but stepping stones to success.

Teamwork, the heartbeat of football, is a value Sarah passionately imparts. Her mentorship transcends the individual pursuit of glory, emphasizing the collective effort required for success. Through collaborative drills, team-building exercises, and a culture of mutual support, Sarah fosters an environment where young athletes understand the true strength lies in their unity.

Beyond the wins and losses, Sarah's legacy is etched in the personal growth of the players she mentors. Many of her protégés not only excel on the football field but also become leaders within their communities. Sarah's story is a living testament to the enduring impact that mentorship, rooted in real-life experiences and a genuine commitment to holistic development, can have on the lives of aspiring athletes. In the realm where tackles meet teachings, Sarah Walker stands as a guiding force, shaping the future one lesson at a time.

4.3 Building Bridges: Community Collaboration

In this chapter, we shine a spotlight on the profound collaborative efforts undertaken by entire football teams, transcending the traditional boundaries of the playing field to make a collective impact in their communities. These endeavors not only redefine the role of athletes but also serve as a testament to the powerful influence of organized sports in fostering positive social change.

4.3.1 The Green Initiative

Witness how the Greenfield Thunder, a local high school football team, spearheaded an environmental campaign known as the "Green Initiative." Comprising players, coaches, and support staff, the team organized regular community clean-up initiatives to address environmental concerns and promote a sense of shared responsibility. From picking up litter in local parks to participating in recycling drives, the Greenfield Thunder's commitment to sustainable practices extended well beyond their time on the football field.

4.3.2 Empowering Minds: Educational Workshops

Explore the impactful educational workshops organized by the Riverdale Rovers, a collegiate football team dedicated to empowering young minds. Partnering with local schools and educational organizations, the players hosted workshops on topics ranging from academic success to career development. Through these initiatives, the Riverdale Rovers not only shared their knowledge and experiences but also inspired local youth to pursue education as a key to unlocking their full potential.

4.3.3 Touchdowns for a Cause: Fundraising Events

Delve into the heartfelt efforts of the Harbor Hawks, a professional football team, as they leveraged their popularity to organize fundraising events for charitable causes. From charity football games to auctions featuring memorabilia signed by players, the Harbor Hawks demonstrated how the sport could be a powerful tool for mobilizing resources and generating funds for community initiatives. The funds raised were directed towards local charities, underscoring the team's commitment to making a tangible and positive impact.

4.3.4 Unity in Diversity

Uncover how these collaborative efforts fostered a sense of unity and pride not only among the players but also within the local community. Through joint participation in community projects, football teams became catalysts for breaking down barriers, forging connections, and celebrating the diversity that defines their hometowns. The shared goals of community improvement became a rallying point, reinforcing the idea that football is not just a game played on a field but a shared endeavor that strengthens the social fabric.

In the realm of community collaboration, football teams emerge not only as athletic competitors but as dynamic agents of positive change. As we explore these real-life stories, it becomes evident that when teams unite for a common cause, the impact extends far beyond the realm of touchdowns and tackles, creating a legacy of shared responsibility, empowerment, and community pride.

4.4 Beyond the Scoreboard: Charitable Foundations

Embark on a journey into the profound impact of charitable foundations established by dedicated football players determined to create enduring change. Within this chapter, we explore tangible instances where the triumphs on the football field evolve into transformative initiatives that transcend the game.

4.4.1 Building Educational Empires

Discover the educational legacies forged by football players who have founded schools through their charitable foundations. One such example is the "Gridiron Scholars Academy," established by former NFL player Marcus Johnson. This institution not only provides quality education but also serves as a beacon of hope for underserved communities, offering a pathway to academic success for aspiring young minds.

4.4.2 Empowering Dreams through Scholarships

Uncover the stories of football players who, propelled by a commitment to education, have set up scholarship programs through their foundations. The "Touchdown Futures Scholarship Fund," initiated by a group of NFL athletes, has become a symbol of the transformative power of education. This program has granted scholarships to countless students, fostering a new generation of leaders who might otherwise have faced financial barriers to higher education.

4.4.3 Tackling Social Issues: Foundations as Agents of Change

Delve into how football players utilize their foundations to tackle pressing social issues. The "GameChanger Foundation," spearheaded by a collective of professional athletes, focuses on initiatives ranging from combating youth homelessness to promoting mental health awareness. Through strategic partnerships and community engagement, these foundations become catalysts for addressing systemic challenges that extend far beyond the world of sports.

4.4.4 Infrastructure for Tomorrow

Explore the architectural impact of football players who, through their foundations, contribute to building essential community infrastructure. From revitalizing local parks to constructing community centers, these athletes invest not only in the tangible structures but also in fostering a sense of pride and unity within the neighborhoods they call home.

4.4.5 A Legacy Beyond the Field

Witness how football players, cognizant of the fleeting nature of their careers, establish foundations as a means to leave a lasting legacy. The "Legacy Builders Initiative," founded by retired NFL star Jessica Martinez, focuses on sustainable community development projects. By leveraging her success on the field, Martinez ensures that her impact endures, creating a legacy that extends far beyond the confines of the football stadium.

In "Beyond the Scoreboard," we delve into the multifaceted ways in which football players channel their success into purposeful action. These charitable foundations emerge as powerful instruments of positive change, leaving an indelible mark on communities and underscoring the idea that the true measure of a player's success is not just in the touchdowns scored but in the enduring impact on the lives of those they seek to uplift.

4.5 Coaching Beyond the Playbook: The Impact of Coach Rodriguez

In the realm of football, where the game is often dissected into strategic plays and precise execution, Coach Rodriguez stands as a testament to the transformative power of mentorship. His influence on young players extends beyond the tactical intricacies of the sport, leaving an indelible mark on the lives of those under his guidance.

Coach Rodriguez's commitment goes beyond the traditional Xs and Os of football strategy. As the architect of a comprehensive mentorship program, he invests time and energy in shaping not just skilled athletes but well-rounded individuals equipped with valuable life skills. Through one-on-one interactions, group sessions, and community involvement, Coach Rodriguez imparts a holistic approach to personal development.

In the crucible of competition, Coach Rodriguez becomes more than a strategist; he becomes a mentor, guiding his players through the challenges of both the game and life. His mentorship program delves into crucial aspects of character building, emphasizing qualities such as resilience, discipline, and sportsmanship.

The impact of Coach Rodriguez's mentorship transcends the field, reaching into the heart of communities. By instilling a sense of responsibility and leadership in his players, he sparks a ripple effect that extends far beyond the final whistle. These athletes, inspired by Coach Rodriguez's guidance, evolve into community leaders, actively contributing to the betterment of society.

Through interviews with current and former players, we gain insight into the profound influence Coach Rodriguez has had on their lives. Many credit him not only for refining their football skills but for imparting wisdom that extends into their personal and professional endeavors. His coaching philosophy mirrors a belief that the skills cultivated on the football field are transferable to the broader arena of life.

In "Coaching Beyond the Playbook," we uncover the untold stories of how a coach's compassion and commitment to mentorship can shape the trajectory of young lives. Coach Rodriguez stands as a beacon, demonstrating that the impact of a coach goes well beyond the wins and losses, leaving an enduring legacy in the hearts and minds of those he guides both on and off the field.

4.6 The Ripple Effect: Transformative Impact Beyond the Field

In this chapter, we delve into the profound ripple effect generated by football players actively participating in community service initiatives. Through extensive interviews with community members, we gain firsthand insights into the tangible impact of these athletes whose commitment to social causes extends far beyond the football arena.

We spoke with residents, local leaders, and program beneficiaries, and their stories collectively illuminate the transformative influence initiated by these gridiron heroes. These narratives underscore the genuine and lasting change instigated by the athletes, who, through their actions, serve as beacons of inspiration for others in the community.

4.6.1 Seeds of Change: Planting the Community Garden

One compelling story emerges from a collaborative effort led by a group of football players who, inspired by a shared passion for sustainability, initiated a community garden project. Through interviews with both players and community members, we trace the journey from planting the first seeds to the flourishing garden that now serves as a source of fresh produce for local families in need. Witness the testimonials of those who have not only benefited from the harvest but have also become motivated to contribute to the initiative, sowing the seeds of positive change throughout the neighborhood.

4.6.2 From Field to Classroom: The Educational Initiative

Another impactful narrative unfolds as we explore a football player's commitment to education. By partnering with local schools and educational organizations, this athlete has become a driving force behind initiatives aimed at improving educational outcomes for underprivileged youth. Through personal accounts from students, teachers, and the players themselves, we witness the transformative power of education and how it serves as a catalyst for change within the community.

4.6.3 A Sheltering Spirit: Homeless Outreach Program

Through interviews with community members and players engaged in a homeless outreach program, we uncover a compelling story of compassion and community support. Football players actively participating in the initiative not only provide essential resources but also forge meaningful connections with those experiencing homelessness. Hear from program volunteers, players, and those who have received assistance, as they share how this outreach effort has created a network of support that extends far beyond the immediate act of giving.

Through these real-life stories, "The Ripple Effect" chapter vividly portrays how the actions of football players in community service resonate deeply, inspiring others to join the cause and contribute to the betterment of society. The impact of these athletes reverberates through the lives of community members, fostering a sense of shared responsibility and a commitment to making a difference.

4.7 The Impact of Community Engagement

Step into the dynamic interplay between football and community, where players forge deep connections with the places that molded them, and communities reciprocate by fervently supporting their local teams. In this exploration, witness the transformative power of this symbiotic relationship, as it emerges as a formidable force for positive change, resonating not only at the local level but also rippling out into broader social landscapes.

In the tapestry of community and football, players recognize the profound influence their roots have had on their journey. Many football stars, acknowledging the support and opportunities their hometowns provided, feel a profound responsibility to give back. This giving back is not merely a philanthropic endeavor; it becomes a reciprocal exchange, a testament to the unbreakable bond between athletes and the communities that shaped them.

As we immerse ourselves in the narratives of these athletes in "Touchdowns and Touching Lives," it becomes evident that the legacy of a football player extends well beyond the statistics of wins and losses. These individuals evolve into change agents, utilizing their influence as more than just players on the field. They become leaders, advocates, and pillars of support within their communities.

These players employ their elevated status not for personal gain, but as a platform to uplift and empower those around them. From initiating grassroots initiatives to collaborating with local organizations, they channel their resources and visibility to address social issues, promote education, and enhance the quality of life for those in need.

What emerges is a powerful synergy between the spirit of community and the game itself. Football becomes a conduit for unity, a rallying point that transcends the playing field. The bond between players and their communities extends beyond game days, permeating everyday life with a shared sense of purpose and pride.

In examining these stories, we witness the profound impact of this symbiosis. The ripple effect of community engagement extends far beyond the local arena, influencing broader societal dynamics. These athletes serve as beacons, inspiring others to contribute, fostering a culture of collective responsibility and compassion.

"In Touchdowns and Touching Lives," we not only celebrate the athletic achievements but also delve into the profound social responsibility shouldered by these football players. Through this exploration, we recognize that their commitment to community transcends the sport, creating a legacy that resonates through the very fabric of society, leaving an enduring imprint that stretches far beyond the boundaries of the football field.

In the world of football, the spotlight often shines brightly on the prowess exhibited on the field. Yet, within the dynamic narrative of the sport, there exists a league of extraordinary individuals who seamlessly weave academic excellence into their athletic pursuits.

5.1 Opening Play: The Dual Commitment

In the realm of American football, there exists a cohort of individuals who transcend the conventional narrative of athletic prowess. These are the unsung heroes of the gridiron – players whose excellence extends beyond the field, seamlessly blending with academic achievements in the classroom.

Meet these remarkable individuals, whose stories echo through the halls of both stadiums and lecture rooms. Delve into the nuanced challenges they face as they navigate the demanding landscapes of both football and academics, executing a delicate balance that requires unwavering dedication and resilience.

Explore the intricate dance between touchdowns and textbooks, discovering the multifaceted nature of their commitments. From early morning practices to late-night study sessions, these student-athletes exemplify the epitome of dedication, juggling the physical demands of the game with the intellectual rigor demanded by their academic pursuits.

Within this intersection lies a narrative rich with lessons. Uncover the hurdles faced and conquered – the late-night struggles with complex equations after an exhausting day of practice, the sacrifices made to attend crucial team meetings while still meeting academic deadlines. These are not just anecdotes; they are testaments to the indomitable spirit that defines the scholar-athlete.

Peel back the layers of this dual commitment, and witness the formation of character and resilience. Beyond the cheers of the crowd and the applause for on-field heroics, lies a silent struggle for academic excellence. These players are not merely performers; they are architects of their destinies, crafting a narrative that extends far beyond the roar of the stadium.

Join us as we embark on this exploration of the simultaneous conquests of the gridiron and the classroom, where the pursuit of victory is not confined to the end zones but extends into the pursuit of knowledge. This is not fiction but a compelling tapestry woven from the real-life experiences of those who have mastered the art of the dual commitment, leaving an indelible mark on the landscape of American football and academia alike.

5.2 Case Study: The Scholar-Athlete Paragon

In this deep dive, we'll examine the real-life experiences of exemplary scholar-athletes, individuals whose commitment to both academic excellence and football prowess has set them apart in the competitive landscape.

Meet the Pioneers

Embark on a journey through the lives of actual scholar-athletes who have become role models for aspiring players. Discover their backgrounds, the challenges they faced, and the remarkable resilience that defined their journeys.

Daily Rituals: A Balancing Act
Explore the intricate details of the daily lives of these scholar-athletes. From pre-dawn workouts to late-night study sessions, gain insight into the disciplined routines they adhere to in order to maintain a delicate equilibrium between academic responsibilities and football commitments.

Time Management Mastery
Delve into the practical strategies employed by these players to effectively manage their time. Learn how they navigate the demanding schedules of practices, games, and academic obligations without compromising the quality of their performance in either domain.

Support Systems Unveiled
Behind every successful scholar-athlete is a robust support network. Uncover the pivotal roles played by coaches, teachers, mentors, and family members in shaping and sustaining the academic and athletic pursuits of these individuals. Explore the collaborative efforts that contribute to their holistic development.

Navigating Challenges: Real Stories, Real Solutions
Face the challenges head-on alongside the scholar-athletes. Through candid accounts, learn about the obstacles they encountered, from demanding travel schedules to academic pressures. Understand the pragmatic solutions they devised to overcome setbacks and emerge stronger on both fronts.

Balancing the Books and the Ball: Personal Strategies
Discover the personalized strategies these scholar-athletes employ to strike a harmonious balance between academics and football. Whether it's utilizing downtime between practices for study sessions or incorporating academic goals into their overall game plan, these individuals exemplify the art of effective multitasking.

Lessons for Aspiring Scholar-Athletes
Extract valuable lessons from the experiences of these scholar-athletes. From the importance of setting realistic goals to cultivating resilience in the face of adversity, distill actionable insights that young readers can apply to their own academic and athletic pursuits.

Reflections on Success: Where Are They Now?
Catch up with these scholar-athletes in the present day. Explore their current endeavors, both within and outside the realm of football. Understand how the skills honed during their scholar-athlete journey continue to shape their lives and contribute to their ongoing success.

This case study serves as a testament to the tangible achievements of those who have seamlessly merged intellectual and athletic prowess, providing a roadmap for aspiring scholar-athletes to navigate their own paths toward excellence.

5.3 Balancing Act: Lessons from the Gridiron and the Classroom

In the real-world stories of scholar-athletes, the intricate dance between the gridiron and the classroom unfolds as a profound learning experience. Their narratives offer a genuine exploration of the tangible life lessons extracted from the simultaneous pursuit of academic and athletic excellence.

Navigating Dual Commitments
As we delve into the lives of these extraordinary individuals, the complexities of juggling two demanding arenas become evident. Discover how these student-athletes navigate the challenges posed by rigorous training schedules, game commitments, and academic responsibilities. The real-world struggles and triumphs illuminate the sheer determination required to balance these dual commitments.

The Discipline Forged on the Field
Explore the symbiotic relationship between the discipline honed on the football field and its direct application to academic pursuits. Witness how the relentless

dedication required for perfecting plays, maintaining physical fitness, and pushing through setbacks instills a profound work ethic that seamlessly extends to the academic realm.

Perseverance Beyond Defeat
In the world of sports and academics alike, defeats are inevitable. However, within the stories of these scholar-athletes lies a testament to the transformative power of perseverance. Understand how setbacks on the field become valuable lessons in resilience, shaping individuals who refuse to be defined by failure but rather embrace it as a stepping stone toward future success.

Strategic Thinking in Action
Football is a game of strategy, requiring players to think critically, make split-second decisions, and adapt to ever-changing circumstances. Witness the transfer of these strategic thinking skills from the field to the classroom. Learn how athletes leverage their ability to analyze situations, anticipate challenges, and collaborate within a team to excel academically and navigate the complexities of life beyond football.

Beyond the Game: A Holistic Approach to Success
As we draw connections between the gridiron and the classroom, it becomes evident that success is not confined to a singular domain. These stories underscore a holistic approach to personal development, emphasizing that the qualities cultivated in the pursuit of excellence extend far beyond the boundaries of sports and academics. Discover how the values of discipline, perseverance, and strategic thinking become lifelong tools for success in various endeavors.

In "Balancing Act: Lessons from the Gridiron and the Classroom," the real stories of scholar-athletes serve as a captivating exploration of the intersection between sports and education. The tangible lessons learned offer a roadmap for young readers, demonstrating that the skills honed on the field become invaluable assets in the broader game of life.

5.4 Coach's Corner: Mentoring Beyond the Field

In this segment, we delve into the practices and insights of coaches who actively champion academic achievement alongside on-field success. Through interviews with these mentors, we gain a nuanced understanding of the pivotal role they play in cultivating a culture of educational excellence within football teams.

Unveiling Mentorship Strategies

Conversations with seasoned football coaches reveal a shared commitment to holistic player development. Coaches prioritize not only the physical and tactical aspects of the game but also the intellectual growth of their athletes. These interviews uncover the various strategies employed to seamlessly integrate academic and athletic pursuits.

Personalized Guidance

One recurring theme is the importance of personalized guidance. Coaches emphasize the unique needs and aspirations of each player, recognizing that a one-size-fits-all approach is inadequate. By understanding the academic strengths and challenges of their athletes, coaches tailor mentoring strategies to ensure each player reaches their full potential, both on and off the field.

Academic Accountability Programs

Several coaches implement structured academic accountability programs within their teams. These programs include regular check-ins, progress assessments, and collaborative goal-setting sessions. By fostering a sense of accountability, coaches empower players to stay on track with their academic responsibilities, creating a symbiotic relationship between scholastic and athletic achievement.

Creating a Supportive Environment

Interviews shed light on the importance of fostering a supportive team environment that values academic pursuits. Coaches emphasize the role of peer mentorship within the squad, where academically accomplished players mentor and support their teammates. This camaraderie contributes to a culture where intellectual achievement is celebrated as much as a game-winning touchdown.

Time Management Workshops
Recognizing the demanding schedules of student-athletes, coaches implement practical time management workshops. These sessions equip players with valuable skills to efficiently balance their academic and athletic commitments. From prioritizing tasks to effective study techniques, these workshops provide athletes with tools essential for success both on and off the field.

Building Lifelong Learners
Beyond immediate academic goals, coaches express a shared vision of building lifelong learners. They understand that the lessons learned in the classroom extend far beyond graduation. Interviews reveal how coaches instill a love for learning, encouraging players to view education as a lifelong pursuit that enhances their personal and professional journeys.

Impact on Team Dynamics
Insights from coaches underscore the positive impact of a culture that values education. Teams that prioritize academic achievement experience improved morale, enhanced teamwork, and greater resilience. By nurturing well-rounded individuals, these coaches contribute not only to the success of their players but also to the overall strength and cohesiveness of the team.

In "Coach's Corner: Mentoring Beyond the Field," readers gain valuable insights into the multifaceted approach coaches employ to nurture both the athletic and academic potential of their players, setting the stage for a future where success is defined by a comprehensive and balanced skill set.

5.5 Beyond the Trophy: Triumphs of the Scholar-Athlete

In the annals of football history, a distinct breed of players emerges—those who have not only conquered the field with their athletic prowess but have gone on to achieve extraordinary success in their academic and professional pursuits. These narratives stand as living testaments to the enduring power of a holistic approach to personal development.

5.5.1 From Field Glory to Boardroom Brilliance

Explore the stories of football players whose names echo in stadiums but whose influence extends far beyond. Learn how these individuals seamlessly transitioned from their sporting careers to excel in the boardroom, leveraging the skills honed on the field to become leaders in various industries.

5.5.2 Academic All-Stars: A League of Scholars
Delve into the academic journeys of these scholar-athletes. Uncover the dedication and resilience that enabled them to not only meet the rigorous demands of their football careers but also to pursue and attain advanced degrees, becoming beacons of inspiration for aspiring athletes.

5.5.3 Impact beyond Touchdowns: Community Leaders
Discover how these former football stars channel their influence into community leadership. Through philanthropy, activism, and civic engagement, they have become champions for positive change, leveraging their platform to address social issues and uplift the communities that supported them during their playing days.

5.5.4 The Transition: Challenges and Triumphs
Examine the challenges faced during the transition from the football field to academic and professional arenas. Realize how setbacks were transformed into stepping stones, showcasing the resilience required to navigate diverse fields and adapt to new challenges.

5.5.5 Mentorship and Legacy
Unveil the mentorship roles assumed by these scholar-athletes. Understand how they pay it forward by mentoring the next generation of athletes, instilling in them the values of hard work, discipline, and the importance of a well-rounded education.

5.5.6 Holistic Excellence: Lessons for Young Minds
Extract valuable lessons for young readers as they witness the holistic excellence achieved by these scholar-athletes. Emphasize the idea that success

is not confined to a singular dimension but is a dynamic and multifaceted journey that encompasses academic, professional, and personal growth.

5.5.7 Navigating Success: Practical Advice for Aspiring Scholar-Athletes
Offer practical advice derived from the experiences of these successful individuals. Provide insights on time management, goal-setting, and the cultivation of a resilient mindset to help aspiring scholar-athletes navigate the delicate balance between academic pursuits and athletic ambitions.

5.5.8 Forever Champions: The Everlasting Impact
Conclude by illustrating how these scholar-athletes, through their enduring success, etch themselves as champions not just on the field but in the broader canvas of life. Their stories serve as guiding lights, inspiring young minds to dream beyond touchdowns and trophies and to embrace the transformative power of education and dedication.

5.6 Halftime Reflection: The Significance of Education

As we reach the midpoint of our exploration into the lives of scholar-athletes, it's essential to pause and contemplate the profound impact that education has etched into the very fabric of these football players' journeys. The convergence of academic pursuits with athletic ambitions is not merely a dual commitment; it's a strategic investment in a future that extends far beyond the painted lines of the football field.

5.6.1 Understanding the Long-Term Benefits
Education, for these players, is more than a means to an end; it's a journey that empowers them with skills, knowledge, and perspectives that transcend the immediate roar of the crowd. We explore the tangible benefits that extend into their professional and personal lives, demonstrating that the pursuit of excellence in education is a cornerstone for building a robust and enduring future.

5.6.2 Beyond the Confines of the Field

As the halftime whistle blows, we shift our focus from the gridiron to the broader landscape of life. The discussion unfolds on how education serves as a foundational pillar, offering these athletes a toolkit for navigating the complexities of the world outside the stadium. From career pursuits to community engagement, education becomes the compass guiding them toward a holistic and fulfilling existence.

5.6.3 Real-Life Testimonials

The narrative gains depth through real-life testimonials from the scholar-athletes themselves. Hear their voices as they recount pivotal moments when education became a game-changer, opening doors to opportunities and shaping their character in ways that extend beyond the physical rigor demanded by football.

5.6.4 Navigating Challenges

Education is not without its challenges, and we candidly address the obstacles these players face. From demanding schedules to the pressure of high-stakes competitions, we explore how these scholar-athletes overcome adversity and use education as a source of resilience and empowerment.

5.6.5 Impact of Mentoring

Coaches, mentors, and educators play pivotal roles in shaping the scholar-athlete's educational journey. Halftime Reflection provides insights into the mentorship dynamics, unveiling the strategies employed by influential figures to inspire a commitment to learning and personal growth.

5.6.6 Inspiring Young Minds

Through compelling stories and concrete examples, we aim to inspire young minds in our readership. The halftime reflection becomes a bridge connecting the experiences of seasoned scholar-athletes with the aspirations of those who are just beginning their own journeys, fostering an appreciation for the enduring value of education.

As we take this halftime intermission, it's not merely a pause in the narrative but an invitation to reflect on the transformative power of education – a force that propels these football players toward a future where success is measured not only in touchdowns but in the lasting impact they make on the world around them.

5.7 Interactive Play: Goal-Setting Workshop

5.7.1 Understanding the Game Plan: Real-Life Experiences
Embark on this interactive journey by delving into the real-life experiences of football players who effectively balanced academic and athletic pursuits. These tangible examples showcase the pivotal role of goal-setting in their overall success, setting the stage for our young readers' own aspirations.

5.7.2 Mapping Your Own Field: Guided Goal-Setting Exercise
Guide readers through a systematic goal-setting exercise, prompting them to articulate both short-term and long-term objectives in academics and sports. This structured approach encourages thoughtful consideration of potential challenges and strategies for overcoming obstacles.

5.7.3 Playbook for Success: Aligning Goals with Passion
Assist young readers in aligning their goals with their passions, drawing inspiration from athletes who discovered academic interests that complemented their love for the game. This section acts as a roadmap, illustrating how education can enhance their athletic journey.

5.7.4 Coaching Insights: Expert Tips on Goal Attainment
Incorporate insights from experienced coaches and educators who have successfully guided young athletes in setting and achieving their goals. Their practical advice on time management, prioritization, and maintaining a positive mindset offers valuable guidance.

5.7.5 Peer-to-Peer Play: Sharing Aspirations
Encourage readers to share their goals with peers, fostering a supportive community. Through peer interaction, young readers exchange ideas, insights, and strategies, creating a sense of collective inspiration and accountability.

5.7.6 Visualizing Victory: Creating Vision Boards

Introduce the concept of vision boards as a tangible representation of goals. Showcase examples of how football players have used vision boards to manifest their dreams, whether on the field or in the classroom. This hands-on activity enables readers to craft a visual reminder of their aspirations.

5.7.7 Reflecting on the Game: Journaling Exercise

Conclude the workshop with a reflective journaling exercise. Prompt readers to record their thoughts on the workshop, insights gained, and any adjustments they may want to make to their goals. This reflective process encourages self-awareness and continuous refinement of their personal game plan.

Through the Goal-Setting Workshop, young readers actively engage in shaping their destinies, recognizing the profound impact of goal-oriented thinking in both academic and athletic pursuits. This hands-on experience empowers them to become architects of their own success stories.

5.8 Closing Drive: The Legacy of the Scholar-Athlete

As we reach the end of our exploration into the realm of scholar-athletes, it becomes abundantly clear that these individuals are not mere players; they are architects of an enduring legacy that stretches far beyond the confines of the football field. Their impact transcends touchdowns and victories, seeping into the very fabric of our society and inspiring generations yet to come.

The legacy of the scholar-athlete is not confined to the trophies on a shelf or the records in a stat book. It is etched into the narratives of lives transformed, dreams realized, and barriers shattered. The story goes beyond the roar of the crowd; it resonates in the halls of academia and reverberates through the professional arenas of diverse careers.

These exceptional individuals, who seamlessly balanced the playbook of academic achievements with the demands of the gridiron, stand as beacons of possibility for aspiring minds. They showcase that success is not a binary choice between the classroom and the sports field, but rather a harmonious blend of both—a symphony of intellect and athleticism.

In the chapters preceding this concluding drive, we delved into the lives of scholar-athletes who navigated the intricate dance of pursuing knowledge and conquering opponents. As we bring this journey to a close, the echoes of their achievements linger, underscoring a crucial message: passion, when coupled with intellectual rigor, knows no bounds.

These scholar-athletes are catalysts for change, breaking stereotypes and redefining the narrative of what it means to be a successful athlete. They serve as role models not just for their prowess on the field, but for their commitment to education, their communities, and the broader world.

As readers close the pages of "Balancing the Playbook: Academic Achievements in Football," they carry with them the indelible notion that the pursuit of excellence is holistic. The impact of these scholar-athletes extends far into the future, as the torchbearers of inspiration for generations to come. Their legacy is not just a chapter in a book but a living testament to the transformative power of passion, discipline, and the unwavering pursuit of both knowledge and athletic greatness.

In the grand tapestry of sports and education, scholar-athletes are the vibrant threads weaving a narrative of triumph, proving that the pursuit of intellectual and athletic prowess is not a trade-off but a harmonious blend that shapes a legacy beyond the end zone.

Step into the pages of football history, where giants roamed the field and their stories continue to echo through time. In this chapter, we uncover the extraordinary lives of gridiron legends who transcended the game, leaving an enduring legacy. From Jim Brown's groundbreaking achievements to Jerry Kramer's resilient journey, each section offers a glimpse into the indomitable spirit that defines these historical icons. Their tales are more than touchdowns and tackles; they are timeless inspirations that have shaped the very essence of American football. Join us as we explore a chapter where the legacies of these titans remind us that, in football, legends never fade.

6.1 Redefining Greatness: The Legacy of Jim Brown

In the storied history of American football, few figures have left an imprint as enduring and influential as Jim Brown. Renowned for his excellence on the field, Brown's impact transcended the game, extending into the realms of civil rights activism and societal change.

Jim Brown, a powerhouse running back, redefined the possibilities of his position during his illustrious career with the Cleveland Browns in the late 1950s and 1960s. His combination of speed, power, and agility set new standards for running backs, earning him accolades that endure to this day.

Beyond the gridiron, Jim Brown emerged as a powerful voice for civil rights, lending his influence to the burgeoning movement during the tumultuous 1960s. In an era marked by racial tension and social upheaval, Brown used his platform to advocate for justice and equality. His commitment to civil rights was not confined to words; he took substantive action, notably organizing the Cleveland Summit In 1967—a meeting of prominent African American athletes addressing issues of racial injustice.

Brown's enduring impact on civil rights goes hand in hand with his football legacy. His groundbreaking achievements as a running back laid the groundwork for future generations of athletes, showcasing the transformative power of sports as a vehicle for societal change.

In this exploration of Jim Brown's unparalleled achievements, we witness a player who not only dominated on the field but also harnessed his influence to confront the challenges of his time. His legacy serves as a reminder that the impact of a sports icon can extend far beyond the confines of the stadium, shaping the trajectory of a nation's history. The story of Jim Brown, the Cleveland Browns icon, is one of athletic brilliance intertwined with a commitment to justice, leaving an indelible mark on the sporting world and the fight for equality.

6.2 The Golden Arm: Johnny Unitas and the Art of Quarterbacking

In the storied history of American football, few players have left an impact as profound as Johnny Unitas, renowned as "The Golden Arm." His contribution to the quarterback position not only transformed the game during his era but also set a standard for excellence that resonates through the decades.

Johnny Unitas rose to prominence in the 1950s and 1960s, a period that witnessed the evolution of the passing game in professional football. Hailing from humble beginnings, Unitas played college football at the University of Louisville, and it was his time with the Baltimore Colts in the NFL where he etched his name into the annals of football history.

What distinguished Unitas was not only his physical prowess but also his cerebral approach to the game. His leadership on the field was unparalleled, with an ability to read defenses and make split-second decisions that became the hallmark of his career. Unitas was not just a quarterback; he was the field general, orchestrating plays with a strategic mind that outsmarted opponents.

Unitas' precision passing revolutionized the quarterback position. His ability to thread the needle with accuracy and deliver the ball with a quick release set him apart. The famous two-minute drill became his trademark, earning him a reputation for clutch performances under pressure. The 1958 NFL Championship Game, often dubbed the "Greatest Game Ever Played," saw Unitas lead the Colts to victory in overtime, solidifying his legendary status.

Beyond the statistics and accolades, Johnny Unitas influenced future generations of quarterbacks. His dedication to his craft, work ethic, and commitment to excellence served as a blueprint for aspiring signal-callers. From Peyton Manning to Tom Brady, the lineage of quarterbacks who admired and emulated Unitas is a testament to his enduring impact on the position.

Unitas' legacy extends beyond the playing field. His football IQ, leadership qualities, and the indomitable spirit he displayed in the face of challenges left an indelible mark on the sport. Even in retirement, Unitas remained an ambassador for the game, sharing his knowledge and passion with aspiring players.

In uncovering the story of Johnny Unitas, we not only explore the career of a football icon but also witness the transformation of a sport through the eyes of a quarterback who became a symbol of excellence. His golden arm and football acumen continue to inspire and shape the narrative of quarterbacking in the NFL and beyond.

6.3 Sweetness Personified: Walter Payton's Unyielding Legacy

In the hallowed history of American football, few figures stand as tall as Walter "Sweetness" Payton, a man whose unparalleled work ethic and indomitable determination not only etched his name in the annals of the sport but also transformed him into a symbol of inspiration for generations to come.
Walter Payton's journey, rooted in a small Mississippi town, burgeoned into a remarkable career with the Chicago Bears. Born on July 25, 1954, Payton's early years hinted at the resilience that would come to define his legacy. His path to football greatness began at Jackson State University, where his prowess as a running back captured the attention of scouts.

Delving into "Sweetness's" career with the Chicago Bears unveils a tapestry of accomplishments that remain unparalleled. From his NFL debut in 1975 to his retirement in 1987, Payton's on-field exploits were nothing short of legendary. He became the NFL's all-time leading rusher, a record that stood for over two decades until it was surpassed. Payton's ability to navigate the field with a unique blend of power, agility, and grace made him a force to be reckoned with, earning him nine Pro Bowl selections and a place in the Pro Football Hall of Fame.

However, Payton's impact extended beyond the turf. Off the field, he embodied the qualities of a true sportsman and a compassionate human being. His commitment to community service, particularly his efforts to promote education and health, showcased a man driven by a desire to uplift those around him. The Walter Payton Man of the Year Award, instituted in his honor, remains a testament to his enduring legacy of philanthropy.

Walter Payton's life was not without its challenges. His battle with a rare liver disease, which ultimately led to his untimely death in 1999, revealed a different facet of his character—resilience in the face of adversity. Payton's courage throughout his health struggles only added to the inspiration he imparted, proving that even in the darkest moments, true greatness shines.

In the corridors of football history, the name Walter Payton resonates as more than a record-breaking running back. It symbolizes the embodiment of sportsmanship, perseverance, and a commitment to making a positive impact off the field. This chapter aims to unravel the layers of "Sweetness's" life, ensuring that his story continues to serve as a beacon of inspiration for young readers, encouraging them to strive for greatness both in their chosen pursuits and as contributors to their communities.

6.4 The Minister of Defense: Reggie White's Defensive Mastery and Spiritual Leadership

Reggie White, hailed as the "Minister of Defense," was more than a dominant force on the football field; he was a game-changer who revolutionized the art of pass rushing and solidified his place as one of the greatest defensive players in NFL history. This section explores White's profound impact on the game and his unique role as a spiritual leader, creating a legacy that transcended the boundaries of the locker room and resonated throughout society.

6.4.1 The Dominant Force on the Field

Reggie White's impact as a defensive lineman was nothing short of transformative. Rising to prominence with the Philadelphia Eagles in the late 1980s, White's exceptional skills and relentless pursuit of quarterbacks became a hallmark of his career. His ability to disrupt offensive plays and consistently deliver quarterback sacks set a standard for defensive excellence.

This section delves into White's unparalleled technique, strength, and strategic acumen, highlighting specific game-changing moments that underscored his dominance. From his tenure with the Eagles to his later years with the Green Bay Packers, White's impact on the defensive side of the ball left an enduring imprint on the sport.

6.4.2 Beyond the Gridiron: Reggie White as a Spiritual Leader

While White's prowess on the field was undeniable, his influence extended beyond the confines of the football stadium. Ordained as a Baptist minister, he embraced his role as a spiritual leader with the same passion and commitment that defined his playing career.

Explore how White's faith played a central role in shaping his character and approach to the game. Whether it was delivering powerful sermons or engaging in community outreach, White's presence as the "Minister of Defense" went far beyond tackles and sacks. His dedication to spirituality not only inspired teammates in the locker room but also left an indelible mark on the broader community.

6.4.3 A Legacy Beyond the Locker Room

Reggie White's impact on the game and society at large continues to reverberate long after his retirement. This section examines the lasting legacy he left as both a defensive powerhouse and a spiritual beacon. White's contributions to the game earned him numerous accolades, including multiple NFL Defensive Player of the Year awards and a well-deserved induction into the Pro Football Hall of Fame.

Furthermore, explore how White's commitment to philanthropy and community service exemplified the values he held dear. Whether championing social causes or inspiring the next generation of athletes, the "Minister of Defense" left an enduring legacy that transcends the boundaries of football fields and echoes in the hearts of those who continue to be inspired by his remarkable journey.

In examining Reggie White's life and career, this section aims to capture the multifaceted nature of his impact, illustrating that true greatness extends beyond athletic prowess to encompass leadership, spirituality, and a profound influence on the communities he touched.

6.5 Beyond the Numbers: Jerry Rice's Enduring Relevance

Jerry Rice's impact on the game of football extends far beyond the statistics that made him the all-time leading receiver in NFL history. While his unparalleled receiving records stand as a testament to his on-field prowess, it is Jerry Rice's work ethic and unwavering dedication to his craft that truly set him apart and continue to define his legacy.

During his illustrious career, Jerry Rice's work ethic was legendary. His commitment to excellence was not confined to game days; it was a daily ritual woven into the fabric of his life. Rice was known for his rigorous training routines, often arriving at the practice field before dawn and staying long after his teammates had left. This extraordinary work ethic wasn't just about physical conditioning; it extended to his meticulous study of the game, a practice that allowed him to anticipate and outmaneuver defenders with precision.

What makes Rice's commitment even more remarkable is its consistency over a lengthy career. From his rookie season in 1985 to his final game in 2004, Rice's dedication to improving himself never waned. This sustained effort wasn't just about personal glory; it was about pushing the limits of what was possible in the sport and setting a standard for excellence that remains unmatched.

Rice's journey from small-town Mississippi to the pinnacle of professional football is a story of resilience and perseverance. Drafted by the San Francisco 49ers in the first round of the 1985 NFL Draft, Rice quickly became a cornerstone of the team's success. His ability to elevate his game in critical moments, particularly in Super Bowls, solidified his status as a clutch performer and a leader on and off the field.

Beyond the accolades and championships, Jerry Rice's enduring relevance lies in his role as a mentor and source of inspiration for aspiring wide receivers. His influence extends to the next generation of football players who look to emulate not just his statistics but also his tireless work ethic and commitment to continuous improvement. Many young athletes entering the league cite Rice as a primary influence, emphasizing his lasting impact on the sport's culture.

In exploring Jerry Rice's journey, it becomes evident that his greatness was not a product of natural talent alone; it was forged through relentless determination and an unyielding commitment to the pursuit of excellence. As young wide receivers aspire to make their mark in the NFL, they find in Jerry Rice a shining example of what can be achieved through discipline, hard work, and an unwavering passion for the game. The enduring relevance of Jerry Rice lies not just in the records he set but in the legacy he crafted—one that continues to shape the future of football.

6.6 Iron Will and Determination - Dick Butkus, the Enforcer

In the landscape of American football, few figures embody the essence of toughness and tenacity as resolutely as Dick Butkus. Renowned for his uncompromising style of play, Butkus left an indelible mark on the linebacker position, transforming it into a symbol of ferocity and defensive prowess. His journey through the gridiron is a testament to iron will and unwavering determination, earning him widespread respect and solidifying his place as one of the most feared defenders in the storied history of football.

Dick Butkus emerged on the football scene in the 1960s, a period marked by the sport's evolution and the emergence of iconic players. Born on December 9, 1942, in Chicago, Butkus's early years hinted at the resilience that would define his career. Raised in the blue-collar neighborhood of South Side, Chicago, Butkus cultivated a work ethic rooted in grit and determination—a reflection of the community that shaped him.

His journey to football stardom began at the University of Illinois, where Butkus showcased an unparalleled passion for the game. As a collegiate player, he exhibited a rare combination of intelligence, athleticism, and a relentless pursuit of excellence. His reputation for hard-hitting tackles and an unyielding presence on the field quickly caught the attention of football enthusiasts nationwide.

In 1965, Butkus made the transition to the professional stage when he was selected as the third overall pick in the NFL Draft by the Chicago Bears. From the moment he stepped onto Soldier Field, Butkus's impact was immediate and profound. His style of play epitomized the essence of a linebacker—ruthless, hard-hitting, and fiercely competitive.

Butkus's ferocity on the field became the stuff of legend. Opposing offenses approached games with a heightened sense of caution, knowing that facing the Bears meant confronting the indomitable force that was Dick Butkus. His ability to read plays, deliver bone-crushing tackles, and instill fear in opponents set a standard that endures in football lore.

Beyond the statistics and accolades, it was the respect garnered by Butkus that truly defined his legacy. Teammates revered him for his leadership and commitment, recognizing the example he set both in practice and on game days. Opponents, while wary of his on-field intensity, couldn't help but acknowledge the unparalleled skill and tenacity that made Butkus a football icon.

As injuries took a toll on his body, Butkus faced adversity with the same determination that marked his career. His retirement in 1973 marked the end of an era, but his impact resonated far beyond the playing field. Post-football, Butkus continued to contribute to the sport, working as an actor, broadcaster, and, notably, as an advocate for player safety.

Dick Butkus's journey is a saga of resilience, passion, and unyielding determination—a tale that transcends the confines of football. Through his ferocious style of play and unwavering commitment, Butkus not only redefined the linebacker position but left an enduring legacy that continues to inspire generations of football enthusiasts, showcasing that true greatness is forged through the crucible of unwavering willpower.

6.7 The Magic Man: Jerry Kramer's Indomitable Path to the Hall of Fame

Jerry Kramer, an unsung hero in the trenches of the offensive line, etched his name in football history through a remarkable journey that culminated in his enshrinement in the Pro Football Hall of Fame. Kramer's story is a testament to unwavering perseverance, unyielding resilience, and the enduring spirit of the game.

Born on January 23, 1936, in Jordan, Montana, Jerry Kramer's football odyssey began at the University of Idaho, where he showcased his prowess as a versatile and tenacious lineman. His exceptional skills didn't go unnoticed, and in the 1958 NFL Draft, the Green Bay Packers secured him as their fourth-round pick.

Kramer's impact on the Packers' offensive line was immediate and profound. As a key member of the famous "Packer Sweep" play, he helped pave the way for running backs like Paul Hornung and Jim Taylor, contributing significantly to the team's success in the 1960s. The Packers, under the leadership of Coach Vince Lombardi, secured multiple NFL championships and triumphed in the first two Super Bowls, with Kramer playing a pivotal role.

Despite his on-field excellence, Kramer faced his share of challenges, including injuries and setbacks. The pinnacle of his career, however, came in the 1967 NFL Championship Game, famously known as the "Ice Bowl." In bone-chilling temperatures, Kramer executed a crucial block that allowed Bart Starr to score the winning touchdown, securing the Packers' victory and a place in football lore.

Jerry Kramer's journey to the Pro Football Hall of Fame was a prolonged one, marked by years of eligibility and near misses. It was a testament to his humility and dedication that he continued to contribute to the sport even after retirement, co-authoring books and sharing his insights as a respected football commentator.

In 2018, the long-overdue recognition finally arrived when Jerry Kramer received his well-deserved induction into the Pro Football Hall of Fame. The honor not only acknowledged his on-field achievements but also celebrated his enduring impact on the game and the values he exemplified.
Jerry Kramer's legacy extends beyond the gridiron. His story, captured in this chapter, serves as a compelling narrative for young readers, offering a glimpse into the challenges and triumphs of a football legend. Through Kramer's journey, readers can glean not only the strategic brilliance of a lineman but also the character, values, and indomitable spirit that define a true icon of the gridiron. Legends like Jerry Kramer prove that, indeed, dedication and resilience create a lasting legacy that inspires generations to come.

Welcome to the captivating world of football evolution, where innovation has become the catalyst for reshaping the very fabric of the game. In this chapter, we embark on a journey through the transformative landscape of football, exploring the ingenious strategies, cutting-edge technologies, and revolutionary training methods that have left an indelible mark on the sport. From the historic shifts in defensive tactics to the tech-driven revolutions in ball design and gameplay analysis, we delve into the dynamic intersection of tradition and innovation. Join us as we unravel the stories behind the game-changing innovations that continue to propel football into a future defined by limitless possibilities.

7.1 The Evolution of Tactics

In the nascent years of American football, the sport bore witness to a remarkable journey in the evolution of both equipment and strategic gameplay. This section delves into the transformative era that shifted the paradigm from leather helmets to the intricate defensive schemes employed in the modern game.

7.1.1 Leather Helmets: A Glimpse into Football's Past

The early chapters of football history narrate a time when the clatter of leather helmets echoed on the gridiron. These rudimentary headgear pieces, symbolic of the sport's rugged origins, provided minimal protection in a game that was still finding its identity. Drawing from accounts of the late 19th and early 20th centuries, we uncover the grit and resilience required of players who stepped onto the field with only leather helmets as their armor.

7.1.2 Pioneering Protective Gear

As the sport matured, so did the emphasis on player safety. This chapter navigates through the pivotal moments when protective gear underwent a transformative shift. From the first appearance of plastic helmets in the 1930s to the innovation of facemasks in the 1950s, we observe how each technological leap aimed at reducing the inherent risks of the game.

7.1.3 Defensive Strategies: An Art Form in Motion

The evolution of football tactics is intricately woven into the sport's fabric, with defensive strategies emerging as a strategic art form. From the classic 6-2 and 5-3 formations of yesteryear to the complex zone blitzes and nickel packages of today, we chart the evolution of defensive schemes. Drawing on real game analyses and expert insights, we uncover how coaches and players continually adapt, utilizing sophisticated strategies to outsmart opponents and secure victories.

7.1.4 Strategic Innovations: Beyond Xs and Os

This section aims to demystify the playbook by examining real-life instances where innovative defensive strategies changed the course of games and seasons. Delve into the strategic minds behind iconic moments, such as the implementation of the 3-4 defense by legendary coach Chuck Fairbanks or the innovative zone coverages that revolutionized pass defense.

7.1.5 The Modern Chess Match on Turf

The chapter concludes by acknowledging the contemporary nature of defensive tactics, acknowledging that the game is a dynamic chess match on turf. From defensive linemen reading offensive formations to linebackers dropping into coverage, the intricacies of modern defensive strategies showcase football's ongoing quest for tactical mastery.

Through a meticulous exploration of football's tactical evolution, readers gain a deeper understanding of the sport's rich history and the strategic brilliance that defines each era. This chapter serves as a bridge between the leather-helmeted pioneers of football's past and the strategic maestros shaping the game's future.

7.2 Technological Advancements
7.2.1 Beyond Leather Balls: The Tech Revolution

The evolution of footballs from the rudimentary leather spheres of the early days to the sleek, high-tech marvels of the present marks a significant chapter in the sport's history. The journey from primitive equipment to aerodynamically designed balls has not only transformed the aesthetic of the game but has also had profound implications for players' techniques and overall gameplay.

In the early years, leather footballs were unpredictable, affected by weather conditions and becoming heavy when wet. The introduction of synthetic materials and advanced manufacturing processes revolutionized ball design. High-tech footballs are now engineered for optimal aerodynamics, providing consistent performance irrespective of weather conditions. This transformation has not only enhanced passing accuracy but has also allowed players to exploit the ball's flight characteristics for more effective shooting and control.

7.2.2 Eyes in the Sky: Video Analysis in Football

The modern football coach's toolkit extends beyond the sidelines, incorporating sophisticated video analysis techniques that have reshaped the way teams prepare and perform. Video analysis has become an indispensable tool for dissecting plays, identifying opponents' weaknesses, and optimizing overall team performance.

Coaches leverage cutting-edge technology to capture every nuance of a match, allowing for in-depth analysis of players' movements, tactical decisions, and strategic plays. This meticulous scrutiny enables coaches to make informed decisions during both training sessions and match preparation. By breaking down footage, teams gain insights into their own strengths and weaknesses, as well as those of their competitors. Video analysis has thus become a cornerstone in developing effective game plans and refining strategies.

7.2.3 The Rise of Wearable Tech

In the quest for peak athletic performance, football has embraced the era of wearable technology, introducing a new dimension to player monitoring, performance enhancement, and injury prevention. Wearable devices, ranging from GPS trackers to heart rate monitors, have become integral to the training routines of professional footballers.

GPS trackers, embedded in players' jerseys, provide real-time data on their movements, distances covered, and intensity of effort during training and matches. Coaches and sports scientists use this information to tailor individualized training programs, ensuring optimal physical conditioning. Similarly, heart rate monitors offer insights into players' physiological responses, helping manage their workload and monitor fatigue levels. This data-driven approach not only enhances fitness but also aids in injury prevention and recovery, contributing to prolonged and sustainable player careers.

The integration of wearable technology exemplifies football's commitment to leveraging innovation for the betterment of player performance, health, and the overall evolution of the sport.

7.3 Training and Fitness Breakthroughs

7.3.1 From the Gym to the Lab: The Impact of Sports Science in Football

In recent decades, football has undergone a paradigm shift in training methodologies, thanks to the integration of sports science. This section explores the profound influence of physiological and biomechanical insights on football training, showcasing how scientific principles have redefined fitness regimens and elevated player performance.

7.3.2 Physiological Precision: Unlocking Peak Athleticism

Sports scientists and fitness experts have meticulously analyzed the physiological demands of football. From understanding energy systems to optimizing recovery, advancements in sports science have allowed for tailored training programs. These programs address the specific physical demands placed on players during matches, ensuring they are better equipped to endure the challenges of a full season.

7.3.3 Biomechanics Unveiled: Enhancing Technique and Preventing Injuries

The marriage of biomechanics and football has ushered in a new era of precision. Analyzing the mechanics of movements, such as kicking and running, has not only improved players' technical skills but also aided in injury prevention. By identifying and correcting biomechanical imbalances, players can reduce the risk of injuries that could sideline them for crucial matches.

7.3.4 Case Studies in Longevity: Prolonging Careers Through Science-Driven Training

Delve into real-life cases where sports science has played a pivotal role in extending players' careers. Whether it's customized training regimens, injury prevention strategies, or tailored recovery programs, these case studies underscore the impact of scientific principles in sustaining peak performance over the long haul.

7.3.5 Teamwide Transformation: Elevating Overall Performance

The integration of sports science is not limited to individual players; it extends to entire teams. Explore instances where football clubs have embraced a scientific approach to training, leading to a collective improvement in performance. This shift goes beyond physical fitness, encompassing aspects such as tactical understanding, teamwork, and mental resilience.

7.3.6 Virtual Reality in Football: A Training Revolution

In the quest for excellence, football has embraced cutting-edge technology, with virtual reality (VR) standing at the forefront of a training revolution. This section explores the transformative role of VR in football training, offering players an immersive and interactive experience that goes beyond traditional methods.

7.3.7 Simulating Real Scenarios: Enhancing Decision-Making Skills

VR technology allows players to step into simulated match scenarios, providing a realistic and dynamic training environment. By facing virtual opponents and experiencing in-game situations, players can hone their decision-making skills under pressure. This innovative approach ensures that athletes are better prepared for the unpredictable nature of actual matches.

7.3.8 Heightened Situational Awareness: Training the Football Brain

Beyond physical prowess, football success often hinges on split-second decision-making. VR training enables players to develop heightened situational awareness, reading the game with greater acuity. This not only benefits individual players but also contributes to a more cohesive and strategically adept team.

7.3.9 Reducing the Gap Between Training and Performance: Practical Applications

Explore practical applications of VR in football training, from strategy sessions to injury rehabilitation. Clubs are utilizing VR to review game footage, analyze opponents, and even allow injured players to participate in virtual training sessions, minimizing the gap between rehabilitation and reintegration into the team.

In summary, the marriage of sports science and virtual reality has ushered in a new era of football training, where precision, adaptability, and enhanced decision-making converge to redefine the boundaries of athletic excellence. As clubs and players continue to embrace these breakthroughs, the beautiful game evolves not just on the field but also in the laboratories and virtual realms where innovation thrives.

7.4 The Globalization of the Game

7.4.1 Scouting in the Digital Age: A World of Talent Discovery

In today's football landscape, the digitization of talent scouting has ushered in a new era of global connectivity. Football clubs now harness the power of technology to cast their nets far and wide, discovering promising players from the most remote corners of the world. The advent of digital platforms and sophisticated data analysis has become a game-changer in the pursuit of identifying and nurturing football talent.

The Impact of Digital Platforms

Football clubs no longer rely solely on traditional scouting networks. The utilization of digital platforms, including comprehensive databases and online scouting platforms, has become integral to the talent discovery process. Clubs can access a vast pool of player profiles, statistics, and performance analytics, streamlining the scouting process and ensuring no hidden gem goes unnoticed.

Data-Driven Decision Making

The use of data analysis has become a cornerstone of modern talent scouting. Advanced algorithms and statistical models enable clubs to assess a player's performance, potential, and suitability for their team with unprecedented accuracy. From tracking on-field metrics to evaluating off-field behavior, technology provides a holistic view of a player's abilities and character, empowering clubs to make informed decisions in their pursuit of talent.

Global Scouting Networks
Football clubs now maintain extensive global scouting networks facilitated by technology. Scouts can remotely monitor players, stream matches, and analyze performance data in real-time. This has not only expanded the talent pool but has also allowed clubs to identify players who may have otherwise gone unnoticed in the conventional scouting process.

7.4.2 Connecting Fans: Social Media's Impact on the Football Experience

As the game on the field evolves, so too does the way fans engage with football, players, and each other. Social media has emerged as a transformative force, shaping the global football experience and creating an interconnected community of enthusiasts.

Real-Time Updates and Highlights
Social media platforms provide fans with instant access to real-time updates, highlights, and in-depth analyses. Whether it's a stunning goal, a crucial save, or breaking news about player transfers, fans can stay connected to the pulse of the game, transcending geographical barriers.

Building a Global Football Community
The role of social media extends beyond match updates. It serves as a virtual meeting ground, where fans from diverse backgrounds converge to celebrate their shared passion. Platforms like Twitter, Instagram, and Facebook foster a sense of community, enabling fans to discuss matches, share opinions, and forge connections with fellow enthusiasts across the globe.

Player-Fan Interaction
Social media has bridged the gap between players and fans like never before. Players use platforms to share behind-the-scenes glimpses of their lives, express gratitude to their fanbase, and even engage in direct interactions. This level of accessibility has humanized football stars and strengthened the emotional connection between players and their supporters.

Global Fandom and Merchandising
The global reach of social media has significantly expanded the market for football merchandise. Fans worldwide can now easily access and purchase team jerseys, memorabilia, and other products, contributing to the internationalization of football club brands.

In essence, the globalization of football through digital scouting and social media has not only transformed the way clubs discover talent but has also enriched the fan experience, turning football into a truly global and interconnected phenomenon.

Conclusion: Embracing the Future

The transformative influence of innovations in football extends beyond altering the dynamics of the game; it shapes the very landscape of the sport and offers a glimpse into its promising future. Examining these revolutionary changes reveals a sport that has continually adapted to emerging technologies and groundbreaking ideas.

In the contemporary era, football stands as a testament to the perpetual evolution of athletic competition. Technological advancements, strategic innovations, and a commitment to pushing boundaries have collectively redefined the way the game is played, elevating it to new heights. These changes not only enhance the present-day spectator experience but also hold the key to unlocking unprecedented possibilities in the future.
The adoption of cutting-edge technologies, from the introduction of state-of-the-art footballs designed for optimal performance to the integration of

wearable tech, has provided teams with a wealth of data to analyze and leverage. Coaches now utilize video analysis tools to break down plays, identify strengths and weaknesses, and fine-tune strategies. Wearable technology, ranging from GPS trackers to heart rate monitors, has become an integral part of player development, offering insights into physical fitness, recovery, and injury prevention.

Beyond the training ground, the globalization of football has been accelerated by digital platforms and the advent of social media. Talent scouting has transcended geographical boundaries, enabling clubs to discover emerging players from diverse corners of the globe. Social media has transformed the relationship between fans, players, and teams, fostering a global community that shares a collective passion for the sport.

As football marches forward into the future, the importance of adaptability and a forward-thinking mindset cannot be overstated. Embracing change and innovation will be essential for players, coaches, and stakeholders alike. The sport's ability to remain dynamic, responsive to advancements, and open to creative strategies will determine its continued relevance and appeal.

In conclusion, the journey of football is not confined to its storied past or the thrilling matches of the present; it extends into a future brimming with potential. By recognizing the impact of innovations and understanding their role in shaping the sport, players and enthusiasts alike can actively contribute to and shape the footballing landscape of tomorrow. Embracing the evolving nature of football ensures that it remains a dynamic, captivating, and enduring force in the world of sports.

Chapter 8: Fair Play, Foul Balls: Sportsmanship on the Field

In the dynamic world of football, where the competition is fierce and the stakes are high, true sportsmanship shines as a beacon of honor. This chapter delves into the inspiring stories of players who not only showcased their exceptional athletic prowess but also demonstrated remarkable sportsmanship, fair play, and genuine respect for their opponents.

8.1 The Handshake Heard Across the Stadium

In the annals of football history, there exists a compelling account of sportsmanship that transcended the fierce rivalry between two teams during a pivotal game. This particular encounter left an indelible mark on the hearts of spectators and players alike, emphasizing the enduring impact of a simple yet profound gesture.

The setting was a highly anticipated match, a clash between arch-rivals that had a history fraught with tension and competitive fervor. As the teams prepared to step onto the hallowed turf, an unexpected scene unfolded. Players from both sides, aware of the heightened emotions and the weight of the impending battle, engaged in an act of unparalleled sportsmanship — the heartfelt handshake.

Before the referee's whistle initiated the contest, each player, with genuine sincerity, extended a hand to their opponents. The handshake ritual was not a perfunctory formality but a tangible expression of mutual respect, acknowledging the shared love for the game that united them despite the rivalry. This simple yet profound act resonated far beyond the immediate context of the match.

Fans in the stands, initially fueled by the spirit of competition and a thirst for victory, found themselves caught in a moment of collective admiration. The sight of sworn adversaries setting aside their differences momentarily to recognize the humanity in one another struck a chord. It became a powerful testament to the essence of sportsmanship, embodying the ethos that football is more than a contest of physical prowess; it is a celebration of camaraderie and shared passion.

As the game unfolded and the intensity on the field reached its zenith, the memory of that pre-match handshake lingered. The players, now engaged in a fierce battle, demonstrated a level of respect that transcended the pursuit of victory. Tackles were robust but fair, and amidst the competitive fervor, moments of empathy and camaraderie punctuated the match.

Post-game, as the final whistle blew, players once again converged at the center of the field for another round of handshakes. This time, however, the gesture carried the weight of shared experience, mutual understanding, and a collective acknowledgment of the game's greater significance. The exchange of handshakes was not a mere conclusion to a match but a continuation of the respect that had defined the encounter from the outset.

This handshake, heard across the stadium and witnessed by thousands, became emblematic of the enduring values that elevate football beyond a mere sport. It showcased that even in the crucible of competition, sportsmanship has the power to bridge divides, foster unity, and remind us all that, in the end, the love for the game unites players and fans in a shared appreciation for the beautiful and noble spirit of football.

8.2 The Assist that Transcended Competition

Within the annals of football history, a poignant moment unfolded, showcasing the extraordinary character of a star player whose actions went beyond the pursuit of victory. In the heat of a crucial game, the spotlight fell on an injured opponent, and it was in this very moment that the narrative of sportsmanship reached new heights.

The protagonist of this tale, a seasoned athlete revered for both skill and sportsmanship, found themselves facing a pivotal juncture. The opponent, a formidable player from the rival team, lay on the field, writhing in pain after a collision that left them incapacitated. The stadium held its collective breath as the referee paused the game to address the unfolding scene.

In a move that defied conventional expectations of fierce competition, the star player approached their fallen adversary with a genuine concern that transcended the confines of the match. Instead of seizing the opportunity to press the advantage, the player extended a helping hand, assisting the injured opponent to their feet. The crowd, initially hushed by the gravity of the moment, erupted into applause at this unexpected display of compassion.

The impact of this act reverberated far beyond the stadium walls. News outlets, fans, and fellow athletes alike were quick to commend the star player for their selflessness. Social media buzzed with admiration, and the clip of this remarkable gesture went viral, underscoring the universal appeal of sportsmanship in football.

This singular act of kindness and empathy not only elevated the player's standing in the football community but also resonated with fans, young and old, who found inspiration in the values of fair play. It became a defining moment in the player's career, immortalized in discussions about not just the talent on display but the character that defined the beautiful game.

As the story unfolded, interviews with the involved players and the coaching staff shed light on the motivation behind the star player's actions. It was revealed that a shared respect for the sport and a belief in the fundamental principles of fair play guided the decision to prioritize humanity over competition in that critical moment.

The narrative of "The Assist that Transcended Competition" serves as a powerful testament to the enduring impact of acts of kindness on the football field. It reminds us that, beyond the tactical maneuvers and strategic plays, the essence of the sport lies in the shared experiences and the values that bind players and fans together. In the heart of competition, this star player proved that true greatness extends beyond the scoreline—it is found in the compassionate moments that define a player's legacy and contribute to the timeless allure of football.

8.3 The Apology Resonating Across the Stadium

In the annals of football history, there exists a compelling narrative that transcends the boundaries of competition, showcasing the profound impact of genuine sportsmanship. This account revolves around a specific player who found themselves in the crucible of a high-stakes game, where emotions ran high, and every move carried weight.

In the midst of the intense match, this player, driven by the pursuit of victory, inadvertently committed a foul against a rival opponent. The collision was unexpected, and the consequences were immediate, but what followed set the stage for a remarkable display of character.

Rather than succumbing to the heat of the moment or engaging in post-foul altercations, the player, realizing the gravity of their actions, took an extraordinary step. With the eyes of the stadium fixed upon them, this athlete demonstrated an unparalleled level of accountability. They didn't wait for the post-match analysis or the referee's decision; instead, they immediately acknowledged the foul, signaling to both teams and spectators alike that the integrity of the game was paramount.

What followed was a moment that reverberated throughout the stadium and resonated with fans beyond the confines of the arena. This athlete, in an unprecedented move, publicly apologized to the affected opponent. The apology wasn't a mere formality but a sincere recognition of the unintended consequences of their actions. It was a testament to the player's character and a reaffirmation of the principles that underpin the sport.

The opponent, initially taken aback by this unexpected gesture, responded with a grace that mirrored the true spirit of sportsmanship. Instead of harboring resentment, the affected player acknowledged the apology, fostering a sense of mutual respect between the two competitors.

The aftermath of this incident extended beyond the boundaries of the field. The players, once rivals engaged in a fierce contest, found themselves bound by a unique connection forged in the crucible of competition and reconciliation. The incident became a catalyst for a lasting bond that went beyond the game, illustrating the transformative power of accountability and genuine remorse in the world of football.

This story serves as a poignant reminder that in the dynamic realm of sports, where passions run

8.4 The Captain's Code of Conduct

Within the rich tapestry of football history, certain team captains have emerged not only as skilled athletes but as paragons of leadership, exemplifying a code of conduct that transcends the boundaries of the game. This section delves into the tangible impact of a team captain whose unwavering commitment to fair play and respect not only elevated the performance of their squad but also reshaped the perception of the entire league.

In the annals of football lore, one such captain took the helm with a distinct vision that extended beyond victory on the scoreboard. Through meticulous dedication and an unwavering belief in the principles of fair play, this leader fostered an environment where sportsmanship was not just a notion but a way of life for the team.

8.4.1 Leadership Beyond the Whistle:
This captain's influence was palpable both on and off the field. In the midst of high-stakes matches, they stood as a beacon of composure, guiding their teammates through moments of tension and adversity. Their demeanor under pressure set a standard for the entire squad, emphasizing that winning was paramount but not at the expense of integrity.

8.4.2 The Ripple Effect:
As the captain consistently upheld the values of fair play and respect, a ripple effect emanated throughout the team. Players began to emulate this ethos, creating a cohesive unit that operated not just as individual talents but as a collective force committed to the spirit of the game. This internal culture, forged by the captain's example, became the cornerstone of the team's success.

8.4.3 Reshaping Perceptions:
Beyond the confines of their own locker room, the captain's influence reached the broader football community. Opponents, officials, and spectators alike took note of the team's commitment to fair play, and the captain's conduct became a benchmark for sportsmanship. The league, recognizing the positive impact of this exemplary leader, underwent a subtle transformation in how it valued and celebrated the essence of the game.

8.4.4 Legacy Beyond Trophies:
While trophies and accolades are temporal, the captain's legacy endured as a testament to the enduring power of leadership. Former teammates continued to carry the torch of fair play in their respective careers, influencing successive generations of players. The captain's code of conduct became a living legacy, shaping the very fabric of the football community long after their retirement.

8.4.5 A Lasting Impact:
In the realm of football history, this captain's legacy stands as a testament to the enduring influence that a commitment to fair play and respect can wield. Their story serves as a compelling reminder that leadership extends beyond skillful plays and strategic acumen—it resides in the unwavering dedication to the principles that define the beautiful game. The captain's code of conduct became a touchstone for captains yet to come, a beacon illuminating the path towards not only victory but the enduring legacy of honorable leadership.

8.5 Beyond Victory: Sharing the Spotlight

In the annals of football history, there are remarkable instances where the essence of the game transcends the pursuit of victory, giving rise to narratives that celebrate not only the prowess of the winners but also the indomitable spirit of the game itself.

8.5.1 The Trophy and the Handshake
Explore iconic moments where winning teams, having clinched the coveted trophy, chose to commemorate their triumph by acknowledging the valiant efforts of their opponents. Through the exchange of genuine handshakes and respectful nods, witness how these victorious teams elevated the spirit of sportsmanship beyond the confines of competition.

8.5.2 The Speech That Resonated
Delve into the post-match speeches of victorious team captains who, instead of basking solely in the glory of triumph, took a moment to express gratitude and admiration for the opposing team. Uncover how these articulate and heartfelt speeches resonated not only with the players but also with fans and the wider football community, reinforcing the values of humility and respect.

8.5.3 Victory Lap, Joint Celebration
Step onto the field as winning teams, after securing a championship, invited their defeated opponents to join them in a symbolic victory lap. Explore the imagery of

athletes, both winners and losers, sharing the joy of the moment, illustrating that, in the grand tapestry of football, triumph is not a solitary pursuit but a shared experience.

8.5.4 The Trophy Dedication

Discover instances where victorious teams, upon hoisting the championship trophy, dedicated their success to the entire football community. Learn how these teams, in their moments of glory, acknowledged that the pursuit of excellence is a collective endeavor, paying homage to the sport and those who contribute to its enduring legacy.

8.5.5 Honoring the Opponents in Victory

Witness the extraordinary scenes where winning teams, amidst their jubilation, took a moment to honor their opponents by forming a guard of honor. Understand how this gesture, often seen in international competitions, became a symbol of mutual respect and recognition of the shared passion for the beautiful game.

8.5.6 Embracing Defeat, Celebrating Effort

Explore instances where winning teams, instead of emphasizing the agony of defeat for their opponents, chose to celebrate the effort, skill, and dedication displayed throughout the match. Understand how this perspective shifted the narrative from victory and defeat to a celebration of the collective pursuit of excellence on the football field.

These documented episodes serve as compelling evidence that, in the realm of football, the celebration of victory is not limited to the conquering team alone. It extends to an acknowledgment of the collective journey, the shared commitment to the sport, and the enduring camaraderie that unites players and fans alike. These instances remind us that, in the end, the true victory lies not just in winning titles but in honoring the essence of the game itself.

8.6 The Referee's Dilemma: Upholding Integrity on the Field

In the intricate world of football, the role of a referee extends beyond mere officiating; it embodies the essence of fair play and integrity. This segment unfolds the true story of a referee who found themselves at the epicenter of a crucial game-changing decision and the resolute commitment to unbiased officiating that ensued.

8.6.1 The Pivotal Moment: A Game in the Balance
In the midst of an intense match, tensions ran high as both teams vied for supremacy. The scoreboard teetered on a knife-edge, and the outcome rested on the next pivotal play. The referee, an arbiter of justice on the field, suddenly found themselves thrust into a moment that could alter the course of the entire game.

8.6.2 The Decision: A Crossroads of Integrity
Faced with a split-second decision that carried significant consequences, the referee weighed the options meticulously. The call in question had the potential to incite controversy, ignite heated debates, and even impact the final standings of the league. Yet, in the midst of the chaos, the referee made a conscious choice to prioritize fairness over expediency.

8.6.3 The Courage to Be Unpopular: Navigating Potential Backlash
Fully aware of the scrutiny and potential backlash that could follow, the referee fearlessly stood by their decision. The choice was not an easy one, as it required a resilient spirit to weather the storm of criticism that often accompanies contentious calls. The referee understood that their commitment to fairness would define the credibility of the sport itself.

8.6.4 The Ripple Effect: Impact on Players and Fans
As the game continued, the consequences of the fair call began to unfold. Players, initially divided by allegiances, acknowledged the referee's impartiality. The decision resonated with fans, even those whose hopes were momentarily dashed. The ripple effect extended beyond the match, influencing perceptions of integrity within the football community.

8.6.5 Preserving the Spirit of the Game: Lessons in Officiating
This episode underscores the critical role that impartial officiating plays in preserving the spirit of the game. The referee's dedication to making a fair call, despite the potential personal and professional repercussions, serves as a beacon for aspiring officials and a reminder that, at its core, football thrives on the principles of justice and equity.

8.6.6 Beyond the Whistle: A Legacy of Integrity
The aftermath of this pivotal moment left an enduring legacy. The referee's commitment to integrity transcended the immediate match, earning respect from players, coaches, and fans alike. This chapter explores how such instances contribute to the evolving narrative of fair play and sportsmanship within the broader context of football.

As readers delve into this real-life scenario, they witness firsthand the challenges faced by referees and gain a profound understanding of the intricate balance required to uphold the integrity of the sport. The referee's journey becomes a testament to the enduring values that form the foundation of football, where fairness is not just an expectation but a non-negotiable cornerstone of the beautiful game.

8.7 The Rising Star and the Veteran: A Mentorship Tale

In the annals of football history, there exists a compelling tale that illuminates the profound impact of mentorship on the development of young talent. This chapter unveils the real-life account of a seasoned player who generously extended a hand of mentorship to a rising star from a rival team, transcending the fierce competition that typically defines the football arena.

The veteran in focus, a respected figure in the football community, recognized the potential of the young talent, not merely as a rival on the pitch but as a burgeoning athlete with the capacity for greatness. The mentorship journey began with a simple conversation, an exchange of insights that extended beyond the technicalities of the game. It evolved into a mentor-protegé relationship characterized by shared experiences, wisdom imparted, and a genuine commitment to nurturing the younger player's growth, both as an athlete and an individual.

Onlookers were not only astounded by the camaraderie that developed between the two players but also by the selflessness of the veteran in dedicating time and energy to guide a competitor. The mentorship extended beyond the training ground, as the veteran provided invaluable advice on navigating the challenges of a professional football career, handling the pressures of media scrutiny, and balancing the demands of personal and public life.

As the rising star honed their skills under the watchful eye of the seasoned player, a transformation unfolded. The rivalry that once defined their relationship on the field gave way to mutual respect and admiration. This mentorship tale became a testament to the notion that, beyond the goals scored and tackles made, football is a community bound by a shared love for the game and a commitment to fostering excellence.

Through interviews with players, coaches, and those close to the mentorship dynamic, this chapter delves into the intricacies of their relationship. It explores the impact of the mentorship on the rising star's career trajectory, shedding light on key moments where guidance proved instrumental. The narrative unfolds with authenticity, showcasing the vulnerability of both mentor and protegé and underscoring the transformative power of mentorship in the competitive realm of football.

In essence, this mentorship tale transcends the conventional boundaries of competition, revealing a narrative that speaks to the unity and interconnectedness that lies at the heart of football—a sport that, at its core, thrives on the shared pursuit of excellence and the passing down of wisdom from one generation of players to the next.

8.8 Kindness Beyond the Game: Football Heroes Turned Community Leaders

In this chapter, we delve into the compelling stories of football players whose commitment to sportsmanship extends far beyond the playing field. These individuals not only exemplify excellence in their athletic abilities but also distinguish themselves as community leaders through dedicated acts of kindness and service.

8.8.1 The Power of Volunteerism: Tackling Issues Beyond the Field

Explore the accounts of football players who rolled up their sleeves to actively address societal issues. From organizing community clean-ups to participating in charity events, these players demonstrate how their commitment to service goes hand in hand with their dedication to the sport.

8.8.2 Building Bridges: Players as Community Connectors

Delve into stories of players who use their platform to bridge gaps within their communities. Witness how these athletes, often hailing from diverse backgrounds, bring people together through football clinics, mentorship programs, and initiatives that promote inclusivity and unity.

8.8.3 Education for Empowerment: Football Stars in the Classroom

Uncover tales of players who recognize the transformative power of education. Discover how they contribute to scholarship programs, establish educational foundations, and actively engage with schools to uplift and empower the next generation, making a lasting impact beyond the confines of the football stadium.

8.8.4 Beyond Borders: International Aid and Impact

Explore narratives of football players who extend their reach globally, using their influence to contribute to international humanitarian causes. From supporting disaster relief efforts to championing global health initiatives, these players showcase how football transcends borders to make a positive impact on a broader scale.

8.8.5 Empathy in Action: Player-Initiated Community Projects

Witness the passion and empathy driving players to initiate community projects that address specific needs. Whether it's establishing youth sports programs, creating safe spaces for at-risk populations, or spearheading initiatives for mental health awareness, these players are making a tangible difference off the pitch.

8.8.6 Leadership by Example: Players as Role Models

Examine how football players, by engaging in community service and acts of kindness, become role models for aspiring athletes. Through their actions, these players inspire the next generation to not only pursue excellence in sports but also embrace the responsibility of giving back to the community that supports them.

As we navigate through these stories of genuine compassion and commitment, it becomes evident that the impact of football extends far beyond the game itself. Readers will gain a deeper understanding of how the values of sportsmanship, fair play, and respect manifest in real-world actions, leaving a lasting legacy that far surpasses the cheers of the crowd or the victories on the field. These narratives serve as powerful reminders that football has the potential to be a catalyst for positive change, with players leading the way as compassionate community leaders.

Chapter 9: Goals Beyond the Goalposts: Goal Setting and Discipline in Football

In the world of football, success is not merely measured by touchdowns, field goals, or victories on the scoreboard. The journey to triumph extends far beyond the painted lines of the gridiron. It begins with a vision, a goal that sets the course for an athlete's trajectory. This chapter delves into the pivotal role of goal-setting and self-discipline, illustrating how they serve as the driving force behind success both on and off the field.

9.1 Setting the Score: The Significance of Purposeful Goals

In the dynamic realm of football, the quest for success is intricately tied to the formulation of clear and purposeful goals. Beyond the visceral thrill of touchdowns and the glory of championships lies a deeper narrative—the narrative of intentional and well-defined objectives that shape the trajectories of football players both young and seasoned. This section delves into the profound impact of purposeful goals, unveiling the tangible outcomes that emerge when athletes set their sights on ambitious yet achievable targets.

9.1.1 The Touchdown Triumph: Goals in the Spotlight

A touchdown is not merely the result of a well-executed play; it is the culmination of a meticulously planned strategy and a player's commitment to reaching a specific target. This segment illuminates how setting the goal of scoring a touchdown serves as a focal point for a player's efforts on the field. Through riveting accounts from football luminaries, readers gain insights into the strategic thinking and sheer determination required to turn the abstract concept of a touchdown into a tangible reality.

9.1.2 Championship Dreams: The Journey to Sporting Eminence

For many football players, the pinnacle of achievement is marked by the pursuit of championship glory. This section unfolds narratives of athletes who set their sights on team success, illustrating how collective goals become the driving force behind grueling training sessions, strategic gameplay, and unwavering team cohesion. The stories presented offer a glimpse into the challenges and triumphs experienced by those who aim not only for personal glory but also for the elevated achievement of championship titles.

9.1.3 Personal Improvement: Elevating the Game, Elevating the Self

Beyond the external markers of success, this section underscores the transformative power of setting goals for personal improvement. It showcases the stories of players who, irrespective of external accolades, set goals to enhance their individual skills, contribute more effectively to the team, or overcome personal challenges. Readers witness how the pursuit of continuous self-improvement becomes a driving force that propels athletes toward excellence on the field and in their personal lives.

9.1.4 From Rookies to Legends: The Evolution of Goals

The chapter unveils a spectrum of goal-setting experiences, ranging from the aspirations of wide-eyed rookies to the seasoned endeavors of football legends.

It explores how goals evolve over the course of a player's career, from the initial dreams of making a mark in the sport to the nuanced objectives of veterans seeking to carve a lasting legacy. The diverse narratives serve as a testament to the enduring nature of purposeful goal-setting throughout a player's entire journey in the world of football.

Through real-life stories, this section illuminates how purposeful goals act as guiding stars, providing direction and motivation to football players at every stage of their careers. Each tale serves as a testament to the profound impact that intentional goal-setting can have on the trajectory of a player's journey, reinforcing the notion that success in football is not just about winning games but about the pursuit of purpose-driven objectives that transcend the boundaries of the playing field.

9.2 The Blueprint for Triumph: Strategies in Goal Setting

In this section, we delve into the tactical maneuvers employed by real football players to craft and fulfill their aspirations. These strategies are not abstract theories but proven methodologies drawn from the experiences of seasoned athletes who have navigated the intricate journey of setting and achieving goals.

9.2.1 Decoding Long-Term Objectives:

The chapter unveils the deliberate and systematic approach undertaken by football players when faced with daunting long-term objectives. It isn't about chasing distant dreams blindly; instead, it involves breaking down colossal goals into manageable, actionable steps. Readers gain insights into how players, from aspiring rookies to seasoned veterans, meticulously dissect their aspirations, allowing them to focus on immediate, achievable milestones. The narrative emphasizes the practicality of this approach, revealing how it transforms seemingly insurmountable objectives into a series of conquerable challenges.

9.2.2 Visualizing Victory:

Goal setting extends beyond the realm of pen and paper; it encompasses the power of visualization. The section elaborates on how football players use the mental canvas to picture success vividly. Through interviews and real-life accounts, readers are introduced to the practice of creating mental images of triumphant moments—touchdowns, game-winning plays, and celebratory scenes. This visualization technique, as employed by athletes, not only bolsters confidence but also serves as a motivational compass, steering them toward their envisioned success.

9.2.3 Learning from the Sidelines:

Setbacks are an inevitable part of any journey, and the chapter emphasizes the role of adversity as a catalyst for growth. Readers explore how football players view setbacks not as roadblocks but as stepping stones toward improvement. Through engaging anecdotes, the section highlights instances where players have transformed setbacks into opportunities for learning and refinement. Whether it's recovering from injuries, facing defeat on the field, or encountering obstacles off the turf, the resilience and adaptability of these athletes serve as inspiring illustrations of using setbacks as springboards for future success.

9.2.4 Strategic Narratives: Real-Life Examples of Triumph Through Goal-Setting:

Embedded within the chapter are real-life narratives from diverse football players, each at different junctures in their careers. These anecdotes provide tangible examples of how strategic goal-setting has been instrumental in their personal and professional development. From rookies making a mark in their debut seasons to seasoned veterans aiming for career milestones, these stories serve as relatable case studies. By weaving together the common thread of strategic goal-setting, the chapter forms a narrative tapestry that resonates with young readers, offering practical insights into overcoming challenges through purposeful planning.

As young readers navigate through the strategies outlined in this section, they are not merely absorbing theoretical concepts but are, in fact, gaining access to the well-guarded playbooks of real athletes. This segment serves as a practical guide, equipping them with the tools to transform their aspirations into tangible achievements through strategic and disciplined goal-setting.

9.3 Discipline on and off the Turf: Navigating Challenges

The journey to success in football is a complex tapestry woven not only with skill and talent but also with a foundational thread of unwavering discipline. In this section, we delve into the critical role that self-discipline plays as the linchpin connecting the ambitious goals set by football players to their ultimate achievements. By examining the lives of real athletes, we gain a profound understanding of the daily rituals, sacrifices, and mental fortitude required to navigate the challenges inherent in the pursuit of excellence.

9.3.1 Daily Routines: The Groundwork for Success

Discipline begins with the establishment of structured daily routines. Through firsthand accounts and insights from professional football players, readers gain access to the meticulous planning that goes into each day. From pre-dawn workouts to post-practice recovery sessions, these routines are not just about physical conditioning but also about instilling a sense of purpose and order, essential for achieving long-term goals.

9.3.2 Sacrifices Beyond the Glory: A Glimpse into Athletes' Lives

Success in football often comes at a price, and this section sheds light on the sacrifices players make to reach the pinnacle of their careers. Interviews with athletes reveal stories of missed family events, stringent dietary choices, and the relentless commitment to training regimens. These sacrifices, while demanding, are essential components of the discipline required to stay on track amidst the numerous distractions that can divert one's focus.

9.3.3 Mental Resilience: Facing Setbacks with Fortitude

Discipline extends beyond physical exertion; it encompasses mental resilience as well. Through the narratives of football players who have faced setbacks, injuries, or challenging periods in their careers, readers witness the indomitable spirit required to persevere. These stories underscore the importance of mental discipline in maintaining focus during both training sessions and the unpredictable journey of life beyond the game.

9.3.4 Training Sessions: A Laboratory for Discipline

Training sessions serve as a laboratory where discipline is tested and honed. Readers gain insights into the intensity of professional football training, emphasizing the dedication and focus required to maximize each session. Athletes speak candidly about the mental discipline needed to push through fatigue, setbacks, and the monotony of repetitive drills, showcasing how these experiences translate into success on the field.

9.3.5 Life Beyond the Game: Discipline as a Lifelong Companion

The importance of discipline doesn't diminish once the final whistle blows. Athletes share how the lessons learned on the field become ingrained in their approach to life beyond football. Interviews with retired players highlight the enduring impact of discipline in their post-playing careers, whether in business, coaching, or community service. The ability to stay disciplined continues to be a guiding force, shaping their ongoing successes and contributions.

Through these real-life stories, "Discipline on and off the Turf" provides readers with a profound appreciation for the unwavering commitment and mental toughness required for success in football. By exploring the discipline cultivated by athletes, young readers gain valuable insights that extend far beyond the sport, inspiring them to embrace discipline as an essential tool on their own paths to achievement.

9.4 Life Lessons from the Gridiron: Transcending Football

Beyond the vivid spectacle of touchdowns and roaring crowds, football serves as a profound classroom where players not only learn the intricacies of the game but also cultivate invaluable life skills. This section of the chapter navigates the journey of athletes beyond the hash marks, illustrating how the principles of goal-setting and discipline acquired on the gridiron become a guiding force in the broader spectrum of life.

9.4.1 Bridging the Gap: Interviews with Retired Players

Delving into the personal narratives of retired football players, this section presents real-life accounts of individuals who seamlessly transitioned from the intensity of the football field to diverse and successful pursuits. Through in-depth interviews, these athletes share insights into the challenges they faced post-retirement and how the foundation of discipline and goal-setting paved the way for their continued success.

9.4.2 Navigating Transitions: Real Stories of Triumph

The narratives underscore the pivotal role of these transferable skills in the players' lives beyond football. From navigating career shifts to pursuing higher education, the stories paint a vivid picture of resilience, adaptability, and the ability to set new goals when the familiar roar of the stadium fades. Readers witness firsthand how the lessons learned during grueling training sessions and high-stakes games become catalysts for triumphs in the real world.

9.4.3 Education as a Touchdown: From Campus to Career

Education emerges as a common theme in these stories, highlighting how football players leverage their skills and discipline to excel academically. Real-world examples showcase players who seamlessly transition from the football field to classrooms, demonstrating that the traits honed through athletics—time management, determination, and teamwork—translate seamlessly into the pursuit of knowledge and academic excellence.

9.4.4 Career Pursuits: Beyond the Helmets and Cleats

The chapter explores diverse career paths embarked upon by retired players, dispelling stereotypes and showcasing the breadth of possibilities. From entrepreneurship to broadcasting, the stories reveal how the discipline ingrained in athletes on the field becomes a driving force in the professional arena. These interviews serve as beacons of inspiration for young readers contemplating their own futures, illustrating that the skills cultivated in sports are not confined to the turf.

9.4.5 Personal Development Touchdowns: Balancing Life's Playbook

Beyond the realms of sports and careers, the narratives also delve into the personal lives of retired players. Themes of family, community engagement, and personal growth emerge as players discuss how the principles instilled by football contribute to their well-rounded and fulfilling lives. Through candid reflections, readers witness the players scoring personal development touchdowns as they apply the same dedication and resilience to their relationships and communities.

In essence, "Life Lessons from the Gridiron" unveils a tapestry of real stories, proving that football is not just a game—it's a transformative journey that equips individuals with skills vital for success in education, careers, and personal development. As readers absorb the experiences of these retired players, they gain a profound understanding of how the discipline and goal-setting inherent in football become guiding principles in the broader arena of life.

9.5 Applying the Playbook: Interactive Exercises for Goal Setting

In this segment, we take a hands-on approach to ensure that the lessons on goal-setting and discipline translate into tangible actions for our young readers. The chapter incorporates interactive exercises designed to empower readers to actively engage with the material and apply it to their personal journeys.

9.5.1 Goal-Setting Worksheets: A Practical Guide
Readers are provided with goal-setting worksheets carefully crafted to guide them through the process of identifying and refining their aspirations. These

worksheets break down the goal-setting process into manageable steps, prompting readers to articulate their ambitions clearly. Drawing inspiration from real-life examples of football players who set and achieved their goals, these worksheets serve as practical tools for translating dreams into actionable objectives.

9.5.2 Measurable Objectives: Turning Dreams into Reality

One of the key lessons conveyed is the importance of setting measurable objectives. This section of the chapter focuses on helping readers develop goals that are specific, measurable, achievable, relevant, and time-bound (SMART). Through examples from the football world, young readers learn the art of crafting objectives that can be tracked and evaluated, ensuring a clear path to success.

9.5.3 Creating Your Roadmap: Navigating the Journey Ahead

Setting goals is just the beginning; the next step is to chart the course to success. Through self-reflection prompts, readers are encouraged to consider the steps and milestones needed to reach their objectives. The prompts draw parallels with the strategic planning that occurs in football, illustrating how a well-thought-out roadmap is essential for navigating challenges and staying focused on the end goal.

9.5.4 Empowering Readers: Applying Principles to Real Lives

The overarching goal of these exercises is to empower readers to apply the principles of goal-setting and discipline to their own lives. By engaging in these practical activities, readers develop a sense of agency, realizing that they have the ability to shape their futures. Real-life stories of football players who transformed their aspirations into reality serve as inspiration, reinforcing the idea that commitment to goals can lead to meaningful achievements.

9.5.5 Beyond Football: Lessons for a Lifetime

These interactive exercises aim to transcend the football field, providing readers with tools they can carry into various aspects of their lives. By mapping their goals, young readers learn skills that extend beyond sports—skills applicable in education, personal relationships, and future careers. The intention is to instill a sense of purpose and determination that will serve them well beyond their reading of this chapter.

9.5.6 Encouraging Reflection: Personal Growth in Action

Throughout the exercises, there is an emphasis on self-reflection. Readers are prompted to consider not only their goals but also their personal strengths, areas for improvement, and the commitment required to achieve their aspirations. This reflective approach encourages a deeper understanding of oneself and fosters a mindset of continuous improvement—a key element of success both in football and in life.

By actively participating in these interactive exercises, young readers are not passive recipients of information but active contributors to their own growth and development. This hands-on approach ensures that the principles explored in this chapter become ingrained in their thinking, setting the stage for a journey of self-discovery, goal attainment, and lasting success.

9.6 Inspirational Quotes and Profiles: Voices of Experience

Embedded within the tapestry of "Goals Beyond the Goalposts" are echoes of wisdom and inspiration drawn directly from the voices of football legends. Interspersed among the narratives and exercises, readers encounter profound and motivational quotes that encapsulate the essence of goal-setting, discipline, and the relentless pursuit of dreams.

Inspirational Quotes:

Tom Brady, Seven-Time Super Bowl Champion:
"Success is not final, failure is not fatal: It is the courage to continue that counts."

Tom Brady's resilience and relentless work ethic have sculpted him into a football icon. His words resonate as a testament to the cyclical nature of success and failure, underscoring the importance of unwavering determination.

Mia Hamm, Soccer Legend and Olympic Gold Medalist:
"Celebrate what you've accomplished, but raise the bar a little higher each time you succeed."

While Mia Hamm's expertise lies in soccer, her philosophy on continual improvement transcends sports. This quote encourages young readers not only to acknowledge their achievements but to use them as stepping stones toward loftier aspirations.

Player Profiles:

Peyton Manning, NFL Quarterback and Five-Time MVP:
Peyton Manning's illustrious career is dissected, revealing the meticulous goal-setting and disciplined approach that propelled him to greatness. From meticulously studying playbooks to maintaining an unwavering focus during high-pressure moments, Manning's journey is a case study in the marriage of ambition and discipline.

Serena Williams, Tennis Phenom and 23-Time Grand Slam Champion:
Serena Williams, though not a football player, shares insights into her relentless pursuit of excellence. Her unwavering dedication to honing her skills and overcoming setbacks serves as an inspirational parallel, emphasizing the universality of discipline in achieving extraordinary goals.

Navigating the Wisdom:

As readers immerse themselves in the anecdotes, quotes, and profiles, they gain not only a deeper understanding of the football world but also a toolkit of practical wisdom. These insights extend beyond the stadium, resonating in the corridors of life where goals are set and discipline is honed.

Life Lessons Beyond the Game:

"Goals Beyond the Goalposts" transforms into more than just a book—it becomes a compass guiding readers toward a future enriched by the experiences of those who have conquered challenges on and off the field. The amalgamation of wisdom and practical exercises empowers young minds to dream expansively, set meaningful goals, and cultivate the discipline necessary to transform aspirations into reality.

In the words of these sports luminaries, readers find not just motivation but a blueprint for navigating the journey ahead. As they absorb the collective wisdom of these icons, they become not mere spectators of the captivating world of football but active participants in the universal pursuit of success and self-discovery.

Chapter 10: A Tapestry of Colors: Diversity in Football

In the vibrant world of football, diversity stands as a testament to the sport's universal appeal. This chapter unwraps the rich tapestry of colors woven into the fabric of football, exploring the stories of players from diverse backgrounds and their profound contributions to the beautiful game.

10.1 Breaking Barriers: Pioneers of Diversity

Step back in time and delve into the untold stories of the courageous pioneers who shattered racial and cultural barriers in the realm of football. These individuals, armed not only with their talent but also with an unyielding spirit, stood at the forefront of a transformative era, paving the way for inclusivity in the beautiful game.

As we journey through the annals of football history, we encounter trailblazers who faced adversity head-on. Explore the challenges that players of diverse backgrounds encountered as they fought for their rightful place on the pitch. From battling racial prejudice to overcoming cultural stereotypes, these athletes forged a path for future generations, demonstrating resilience that echoes through the decades.

Discover the narratives of those who not only showcased exceptional skill but also served as beacons of hope and change. Their journeys extend beyond the stadiums, leaving an indelible mark on the sport and society at large. Learn how these pioneers, through their unwavering commitment and determination, forced football to confront its biases and evolve into a more inclusive and diverse space.

Their legacies resonate in the stories of modern-day football stars, illustrating that the strides made by these pioneers were not merely steps but leaps toward a more equitable future. The echoes of their achievements reverberate through generations, inspiring players of today to embrace diversity, appreciate differences, and continue the fight against discrimination both on and off the field.

10.2 Global Icons: International Stars on the Rise

In this chapter, we delve into the captivating stories of international football stars whose journeys have transcended borders, contributing to the globalization and enrichment of the beautiful game. These athletes, originating from diverse corners of the globe, have not only showcased exceptional skill on the field but have also navigated the challenges associated with adapting to new cultures and football styles.

10.2.1 The Global Footprints

Let's trace the global footprints of football icons who emerged from countries with distinct footballing traditions. From the samba-infused rhythms of Brazil to the tiki-taka mastery of Spain, discover how players have seamlessly integrated these unique styles into their gameplay, creating a dynamic fusion that captivates fans worldwide.

10.2.2 Navigating Cultural Nuances

The journey of international football stars involves more than just adapting to tactical variations. It's a narrative of navigating cultural nuances, language barriers, and the intricacies of life in a foreign land. Explore how these athletes, with resilience and open-mindedness, embraced diversity, fostering a deeper connection with their teammates, coaches, and fans.

10.2.3 The Clash of Playing Philosophies

Dive into the intricacies of the clash of playing philosophies as players transition from one footballing culture to another. Witness the evolution of playing styles and strategies, as international stars bring their unique flair to teams, enriching the global football landscape with a tapestry of skills and techniques.

10.2.4 Pioneers of Cross-Cultural Integration

Celebrate the pioneers who paved the way for cross-cultural integration in football. These trailblazers not only excelled in their craft but also became ambassadors for unity, breaking down stereotypes and fostering a sense of interconnectedness among players and fans across continents.

10.2.5 Challenges and Triumphs

Behind the glitz and glamour lies a journey marked by challenges and triumphs. From homesickness to adapting to new training regimens, explore the personal and professional hurdles that international stars faced on their paths to success. Their stories serve as beacons of inspiration for aspiring players navigating similar challenges.

10.2.6 Impact Beyond the Field

Examine the impact of international football stars beyond the confines of the field. Through their global influence, these players become cultural ambassadors, shaping perceptions and bridging gaps between nations. Discover how their popularity contributes to the universal appeal of football, turning the sport into a shared language spoken by millions.

10.2.7 Legacy and Inspiration

Conclude by exploring the lasting legacy and inspiration left by these international football stars. From fostering cultural exchange to inspiring the next generation of players, their contributions extend far beyond the duration of their careers, leaving an indelible mark on the global football community.

In unraveling these narratives, we gain a profound appreciation for the transformative power of international football, where diversity not only enhances the game but becomes a source of strength, unity, and inspiration for fans worldwide.

10.3 Cultural Celebrations: Traditions on the Pitch

Step onto the hallowed grounds of football pitches worldwide, and you'll find a captivating tapestry of cultural celebrations and traditions that adds a unique and vibrant dimension to the beautiful game. These expressions of heritage and identity extend far beyond the tactical plays and strategic maneuvers, shaping the very soul of football.

10.3.1 Goal Celebrations: A Cultural Kaleidoscope

Every goal scored is not merely a numerical addition to the scoreboard; it's a moment for players to showcase their roots. Witness the exuberant goal celebrations that draw inspiration from cultural rituals. From dance forms deeply embedded in African traditions to gestures paying homage to ancestral customs, these expressions reveal the rich diversity etched into the sport.

Take, for instance, the iconic goal celebration of Senegalese forward Sadio Mané. His post-goal dance, inspired by the traditional "Sabar" dance of the Wolof people, not only electrifies the stadium but also serves as a powerful connection to his Senegalese heritage.

10.3.2 Pre-match Routines: Rituals and Superstitions

Before the referee's first whistle, the rituals and superstitions of footballers unfold, each a testament to cultural influence. Players, steeped in their own traditions, engage in pre-match routines that go beyond the realm of mere habit. These rituals serve as a source of comfort, inspiration, and a way to connect with their cultural roots.

Consider the Haka performed by the New Zealand national rugby team—the All Blacks—a ritual that has transcended rugby to influence other sports. While not exclusive to football, the concept of pre-game rituals is universal. Players might engage in personal or team rituals, each providing a glimpse into the diverse cultural backgrounds they carry onto the pitch.

10.3.3 The Fusion of Cultures: Global Icons on Display

In the modern era of football, where players traverse continents to play for clubs and nations, we witness a fusion of cultures on the pitch. Global icons seamlessly blend elements from different traditions, creating a harmonious spectacle that reflects the multicultural nature of the sport.

A striking example is the celebration of diversity during major international tournaments. Teams don jerseys adorned with cultural motifs, and players exchange jerseys as a symbol of mutual respect, showcasing how football serves as a bridge connecting diverse cultures on a shared playing field.

10.3.4 From Chants to Instruments: The Soundtrack of Diversity

Cultural celebrations extend beyond visual expressions to the auditory realm. The terraces resonate with a cacophony of chants, songs, and even traditional instruments that echo the diverse backgrounds of the players and the fans. The stadium becomes a melting pot of sound, with each note and rhythm contributing to the vibrant cultural mosaic that defines football as a global phenomenon.

As we explore these cultural celebrations on the pitch, we uncover a dimension of football that transcends the boundaries of sport, weaving together a narrative of unity in diversity. The football pitch emerges not only as a battleground for competition but also as a canvas for the world's cultures to paint their stories in every match, goal, and celebration.

10.4 Embracing Differences: Unity in the Locker Room

Step inside the sacred confines of the locker room, a realm where the essence of a team's unity often finds its most authentic expression. In the world of football, this space is a microcosm of the diverse backgrounds that players bring to the pitch. The stories that unfold behind these closed doors reveal not only the shared pursuit of victory but also the genuine camaraderie that transcends cultural and racial divides.

Within the locker room, a symphony of languages, customs, and rituals creates a harmonious blend, fostering an environment where differences are not only acknowledged but embraced. Take, for instance, the 2018 French national football team, a diverse ensemble of players representing various ethnicities and cultural roots. Their journey to winning the FIFA World Cup highlighted how unity in diversity can be a potent force on the grandest stage.

In the heart of the locker room, players share more than just a common goal – they share life experiences, cultural nuances, and personal stories. These interactions create bonds that extend beyond the field, knitting together a tightly woven fabric of understanding and respect. Coaches and team managers play a pivotal role in fostering this atmosphere, recognizing that a team's strength lies not only in the skill of its players but also in the diversity of perspectives they bring.

Heartwarming anecdotes abound, illustrating how players from disparate backgrounds form an inseparable brotherhood. From players exchanging traditional greetings to sharing culinary delights reflective of their diverse heritages, the locker room becomes a melting pot of cultural exchange. Such interactions go beyond mere symbolism; they contribute to a collective mindset that transcends the challenges posed by cultural and racial differences.

The impact of this unity resonates far beyond the confines of the locker room. On the field, teams with diverse rosters often display a versatility that confounds opponents. The fusion of playing styles and strategic approaches drawn from various footballing cultures creates a dynamic on-field synergy that is hard to predict and counter. The celebrated success of teams like Barcelona, known for their multicultural squad, underlines the strategic advantage that diversity can confer.

Off the field, these diverse teams become ambassadors for unity and inclusivity. Their success stories inspire fans globally, reinforcing the idea that football is a universal language that speaks to people regardless of their background. The journey from locker room camaraderie to success on the field becomes a testament to the transformative power of embracing differences.

In the locker room, as in the broader world, the celebration of diversity is not a mere formality; it is a deliberate and conscious effort to leverage the strength that comes from acknowledging and respecting each other's unique qualities. These stories from the inner sanctum of football teams reveal that unity forged in diversity is not just a slogan but a lived experience, a testament to the beautiful game's capacity to unite beyond the boundaries of race, culture, and nationality.

10.5 Beyond Borders: Football Diplomacy and Unity

In the world of football, remarkable instances abound where the sport transcends the boundaries of politics, fostering diplomacy and unity on an international stage. This section unveils real stories of football's impact as a catalyst for positive change and global unity.

10.5.1 Historic Matches Defusing Political Tensions:

Explore the gripping accounts of historic football matches that played a pivotal role in defusing political tensions between nations. From the "Football War" resolution between Honduras and El Salvador in 1969 to the "Diplomatic Football Match" between Iran and the United States during the 1998 World Cup qualifiers, witness how the beautiful game has been utilized to ease geopolitical strains.

10.5.2 Peaceful Collaborations Beyond the Pitch:

Delve into collaborative efforts initiated by football organizations, clubs, and players aimed at fostering peace in conflict-ridden regions. Discover how initiatives like the "Football for Peace" program in the Middle East and the "Goal Click Refugees" project have utilized the sport's universal language to bring people together, fostering understanding and cooperation beyond the football pitch.

10.5.3 Football as a Bridge: Diplomatic Exchanges:

Explore instances where football has served as a bridge for diplomatic exchanges between nations. Learn about football-related diplomatic missions and exchanges that have facilitated dialogue and understanding. Realize the power of a shared passion for football in breaking down barriers and creating opportunities for meaningful diplomatic engagement.

10.5.4 The Impact of International Football Tournaments:

Investigate the impact of international football tournaments in promoting unity and diplomacy. From the joint bid by South Korea and Japan for the 2002 World Cup to the collaborative hosting of the 2026 World Cup by the United States, Canada, and Mexico, witness how football events can serve as platforms for diplomatic collaboration, promoting unity and shared values on a global scale.

10.5.5 Football Stars as Ambassadors for Peace:

Discover the roles played by football stars as ambassadors for peace and goodwill. Explore instances where renowned players have used their influence to advocate for peace, humanitarian causes, and diplomacy. From UNICEF ambassadors to involvement in global charity initiatives, football stars are increasingly leveraging their fame for positive change on a global level.

In this exploration of football diplomacy, witness how the sport extends beyond the pitch, becoming a potent instrument for fostering unity, dialogue, and positive change in a world often marked by geopolitical tensions. These real stories underscore football's unique ability to bring nations together, transcending political divides in the pursuit of a common goal — the love for the beautiful game.

10.6 Women in Football: Breaking Gender Stereotypes

In the realm of football, the narrative of gender equality has gained momentum with the emergence of trailblazing women who have not only broken through the glass ceiling but have left an indelible mark on the beautiful game. This section sheds light on the real-life stories of female players, coaches, and influencers whose contributions have been pivotal in advancing women's football and championing inclusivity.

10.6.1 Pioneering Players: Changing the Game

Explore the journeys of pioneering female players who blazed a trail in a historically male-dominated sport. From the gritty determination of the early trailblazers to the skillful prowess of contemporary athletes, witness how these women transformed perceptions and shattered stereotypes on the field.

10.6.2 Coaching Champions: Women on the Sidelines

Delve into the stories of women who have donned the coaching hat, steering teams to victory and challenging the notion that coaching is an exclusively male domain. Discover the challenges they faced, the strategies they employed, and the victories that underscore their influence in shaping the next generation of footballers.

10.6.3 Off the Pitch Influence: Women in Football Leadership

Beyond the playing field and sidelines, learn about the women who have assumed leadership roles in football's boardrooms and administrative bodies. Uncover the stories of those who have broken through corporate barriers, contributing to the strategic development and growth of women's football at both regional and global levels.

10.6.4 Bridging the Pay Gap: Advocates for Equality

Delve into the efforts of women who have been at the forefront of advocating for gender equality in football, particularly concerning wage disparities. Learn about the initiatives and movements that aim to bridge the pay gap between male and female players, and the individuals who have been instrumental in driving this dialogue forward.

10.6.5 Beyond Boundaries: International Icons

Explore the narratives of women who have transcended national boundaries to become international icons in women's football. These players have not only achieved success on the pitch but have become ambassadors for the sport, inspiring young girls globally to dream big and break through barriers.

10.6.6 Overcoming Adversity: Triumphs Against the Odds

Hear the stories of female footballers who faced adversity on multiple fronts, from societal prejudices to the struggles of balancing personal and professional life. Discover how resilience, determination, and passion enabled them to triumph against the odds, becoming beacons of inspiration for aspiring female athletes.

10.6.7 Grassroots Impact: Cultivating the Future of Women's Football

Examine the stories of women who are making a difference at the grassroots level, fostering the growth of women's football from the ground up. These individuals are involved in community programs, youth development initiatives, and grassroots organizations, sowing the seeds for a more inclusive and diverse future in the sport.

10.6.8 Media Mavericks: Women Shaping Football Narratives

Highlight the contributions of women who have made strides in sports journalism and media, shaping the narratives around football. From insightful commentary to breaking down stereotypes through storytelling, these women have played a crucial role in altering the perception of women's football in the public eye.

As we navigate the stories of these remarkable women, it becomes evident that their impact extends far beyond the confines of the football pitch. They are architects of change, challenging norms, and ushering in a new era where gender is no longer a barrier but a celebration of diverse talent and passion for the beautiful game.

10.7 Inspirational Journeys: From Adversity to Triumph

In this chapter, we uncover the compelling narratives of football players who navigated through not only the inherent challenges of the game but also the formidable barriers of societal prejudices. These stories serve as powerful testaments to the unwavering spirit of individuals whose resilience, talent, and determination triumphed over discrimination.

10.7.1 Eusebio - Breaking Racial Barriers:

Journey back to the era when racial prejudice cast a long shadow over football. Explore the life of Eusebio, a legendary Portuguese footballer of Mozambican descent, who rose to prominence in the 1960s. Despite facing racial bias, Eusebio's remarkable talent and goal-scoring prowess not only shattered stereotypes but also earned him widespread acclaim, leaving an indelible mark on the sport.

10.7.2 Lilian Thuram - A Defender Beyond the Field:

Delve into the story of Lilian Thuram, a French World Cup-winning defender of Guadeloupean origin. Thuram not only showcased exceptional defensive skills on the field but also became a prominent anti-racism advocate off the pitch. His journey stands as a powerful example of how footballers can leverage their influence to address societal issues and promote inclusivity.

10.7.3 Mario Balotelli - Confronting Stereotypes:

Explore the tumultuous yet inspiring career of Mario Balotelli, an Italian striker of Ghanaian descent. Balotelli faced racial discrimination throughout his career but responded with resilience and skill. His journey reflects the ongoing struggle against racial stereotypes in football, inspiring a new generation to challenge societal prejudices.

10.7.4 Marta - Paving the Way for Women's Football:

Turn the spotlight to Marta, a Brazilian forward widely regarded as one of the greatest female footballers. Enduring skepticism and gender bias, Marta's skill and determination have not only elevated her as a football icon but have also played a pivotal role in breaking down barriers for women in the sport. Her story serves as a beacon for aspiring female players globally.

10.7.5 Collin Martin - Embracing Authenticity:

Explore the journey of Collin Martin, an openly gay American professional soccer player. In a landscape where LGBTQ+ representation in sports can be challenging, Martin's courage to embrace his authentic self has made him a trailblazer. His story sheds light on the importance of inclusivity and acceptance in the world of football.

10.7.6 Kalidou Koulibaly - Rising Above Adversity:

Dive into the narrative of Kalidou Koulibaly, a Senegalese center-back playing in Serie A. Koulibaly faced racial abuse on the field, yet his stellar performances and dignified response have garnered widespread admiration. His journey underscores the ongoing battle against racism in football and the resilience required to rise above adversity.

10.7.7 Hope Solo - Goalkeeping Against Gender Bias:

Uncover the challenges faced by Hope Solo, a highly accomplished American goalkeeper. Solo not only overcame gender bias in a predominantly male-dominated sport but also became a vocal advocate for equal pay and opportunities for female players. Her journey exemplifies the struggles and triumphs of women pushing for equality in football.
These stories of triumph over adversity underscore the transformative power of football, proving that the sport is not only a battleground for goals but also a stage where individuals can defy societal prejudices and emerge as champions of change.

10.8 Voices of Change: Advocacy in Football

In this pivotal section, we turn our attention to the profound impact football players have made as advocates for social justice and equality. The stories within these lines are not products of imagination but reflections of the real-world contributions of athletes who've harnessed the power of their platforms to drive positive change.

10.8.1 The Kaepernick Effect: Taking a Knee for Justice

In 2016, NFL quarterback Colin Kaepernick took a knee during the national anthem to protest racial injustice and police brutality. This singular act sparked a movement, leading to widespread discussions on systemic racism and inequality both within and outside the sports world.

10.8.2 Megan Rapinoe: A Champion On and Off the Pitch

Renowned soccer player Megan Rapinoe has been an unapologetic advocate for gender equality. From championing equal pay for women in sports to advocating for LGBTQ+ rights, Rapinoe's activism has elevated her influence beyond the soccer field.

10.8.3 Marcus Rashford: Tackling Child Food Poverty

Manchester United and England forward Marcus Rashford has become a symbol of advocacy against child food poverty. His impactful campaigning led to policy changes in the UK, highlighting how athletes can directly influence governmental decisions.

10.8.4 LeBron James: More Than an Athlete

NBA superstar LeBron James has consistently used his platform to address social issues, particularly focusing on racial equality and educational opportunities. His philanthropic initiatives, including the LeBron James Family Foundation, aim to uplift communities and empower the next generation.

10.8.5 The Rise of Athlete Activism: From Ali to the Present

Delve into the historical context of athlete activism, tracing its roots from Muhammad Ali's stance against the Vietnam War to the present-day, where athletes across various sports continue to raise their voices for justice and equality.

10.8.6 The Global Impact of Say No To Racism Campaigns

Explore the initiatives by football governing bodies, including FIFA and UEFA, to combat racism in the sport. From anti-racism campaigns to strict measures against discriminatory behavior, football organizations are actively working to create a more inclusive and respectful environment.

10.8.7 Beyond Borders: Football Diplomacy and Social Change

Uncover instances where football has played a role in diplomatic efforts and social change beyond the playing field. From joint initiatives between conflicting nations to campaigns addressing global challenges, football emerges as a powerful force for positive transformation.

10.8.8 Grassroots Movements: From Neighborhoods to Nations

Highlight the impact of grassroots movements led by football players. These initiatives, often rooted in the communities where athletes grew up, aim to address local issues, demonstrating how change can start from the ground up.

10.8.9 The Challenges and Triumphs of LGBTQ+ Athletes

Shed light on the journeys of LGBTQ+ football players who've navigated the challenges of discrimination and stigma. Celebrate their triumphs as they contribute to creating a more inclusive and accepting environment within the world of football.

10.8.10 The Continued Evolution of Advocacy in Football

Reflect on the evolving landscape of advocacy in football and how athletes continue to use their voices to amplify social causes. From online activism to community engagement, explore the multifaceted ways in which football players contribute to a more just and equal society.

In this exploration of advocacy in football, these real-life narratives stand as testament to the transformative potential of sports. The impact of athletes transcends stadiums, influencing societal conversations and propelling us toward a more equitable future.

10.9 Future Stars: Nurturing Diversity in Youth Football

In the dynamic landscape of youth football, initiatives and programs have emerged with a dedicated focus on fostering diversity, ensuring that the next generation of players embraces and celebrates differences. As we examine these efforts, a clearer picture emerges of the deliberate steps being taken to nurture inclusivity within the realms of the beautiful game.

10.9.1 Grassroots Movements: Cultivating Talent from the Ground Up

At the grassroots level, community-driven initiatives are sowing the seeds of diversity in youth football. Local clubs and organizations are investing in outreach programs that actively seek talent from diverse backgrounds. These movements not only identify young players with potential but also emphasize the importance of inclusivity and equal opportunity from the earliest stages of a player's development.

10.9.2 Academies with a Global Vision

Across the globe, football academies are adopting a proactive approach to diversity. These academies, often associated with professional clubs, are designed not only to refine football skills but also to instill values of respect, teamwork, and cultural understanding. By bringing together young talents from various ethnicities, socio-economic backgrounds, and cultures, these academies mirror the global nature of the sport.

10.9.3 Scholarship Programs: Bridging Gaps and Creating Opportunities

Recognizing that socio-economic factors can be barriers to participation, scholarship programs have been established to provide opportunities for talented youngsters irrespective of their financial circumstances. These programs aim to bridge gaps, ensuring that the football field becomes a level playing ground where merit and passion prevail over financial constraints.

10.9.4 Diversity Training for Coaches and Mentors

An integral part of nurturing diversity in youth football involves preparing coaches and mentors to embrace and effectively guide a diverse group of young players. Training programs emphasize cultural competency, sensitivity, and awareness, equipping coaches with the tools needed to create an inclusive and supportive environment for players from all walks of life.

10.9.5 Global Exchanges and Tournaments

Initiatives such as global youth football exchanges and tournaments provide young players with the opportunity to interact with peers from different countries and backgrounds. These experiences not only enhance their football skills but also foster cultural exchange, breaking down stereotypes, and building lasting connections among aspiring football stars from diverse cultures.

10.9.6 Community Engagement and Outreach
Beyond formalized programs, community engagement and outreach efforts are key to ensuring that football remains accessible to all. Clubs, organizations, and professional players actively engage with local communities, organizing events, workshops, and coaching clinics to inspire and nurture talent within neighborhoods where diversity is a strength.

10.9.7 Inclusive Policies in Youth Football Leagues

Recognizing the importance of representation at all levels, youth football leagues are implementing inclusive policies. These policies encourage equal participation, regardless of gender, race, or socio-economic background, reinforcing the idea that diversity is not only celebrated but actively sought after for the betterment of the sport.

By delving into these initiatives, it becomes evident that the future of football is being shaped by deliberate actions aimed at cultivating a diverse and inclusive community of players. These efforts ensure that the football pitches of tomorrow reflect the rich tapestry of the world, where differences are not just tolerated but celebrated as integral to the essence of the beautiful game.

10.10 Unity Through the Beautiful Game

In the final exploration of this chapter, we turn our attention to the profound impact of football as a unifying force across the globe. The beautiful game, with its intricate tapestry of diverse players and fervent fans, stands as a testament to its unique ability to transcend cultural, racial, and societal boundaries.

Football, more than just a sport, becomes a universal language spoken by millions. As we reflect on the global stage of this beloved game, we witness its power to bridge gaps, foster understanding, and create connections that reach far beyond the confines of the pitch.

10.10.1 Breaking Down Borders

Through a myriad of international tournaments, club competitions, and friendly matches, football becomes a catalyst for breaking down borders. Players from different nations, with varied backgrounds and life experiences, converge on the field with a shared passion for the game. In these moments, nationalities fade into the background, giving way to a collective celebration of skill, teamwork, and the sheer joy of competition.

10.10.2 A Shared Spectacle

Football matches, whether played in a local park or on a grand international stage, draw together diverse crowds of spectators. The shared experience of witnessing a goal, the collective gasp at a near miss, and the jubilation of victory create a unique camaraderie among fans. In these moments, differences dissolve, and a shared identity as football enthusiasts takes precedence.

10.10.3 Social Impact Beyond the Field

Beyond the confines of stadiums, football leaves an indelible mark on communities worldwide. Initiatives such as street football programs, community leagues, and football-driven charitable efforts bring people together, fostering a sense of belonging and shared purpose. The sport becomes a vehicle for social change, addressing issues ranging from inequality to poverty, uniting communities in pursuit of common goals.

10.10.4 A Stage for Advocacy

Prominent players and football organizations leverage the sport's global platform to advocate for important societal issues. From campaigns against racism to initiatives supporting environmental sustainability, football serves as a stage for impactful advocacy. Players, once seen solely as athletes, emerge as influential voices championing positive change.

10.10.5 A Pathway to Diplomacy

Football diplomacy, exemplified by historic matches and collaborative events, showcases the potential for the sport to transcend political tensions. Nations find common ground on the pitch, fostering dialogue and understanding that extends beyond the realm of sports.

In conclusion, as we delve into these real stories of diversity in football, it becomes evident that the sport is not merely a pastime but a force that unites people across borders, cultures, and backgrounds. The beautiful game, with its inherent ability to inspire, entertain, and bring joy, serves as a living testament to the enduring truth that unity in diversity is not just a slogan but a reality within the global embrace of football.